8 M[...]
20[...]

Michéle

&

Russell

With best Wishes

Elliot [signature]

The Pater
My Father, My Judaism, My Childlessness

The Pater is a searingly personal gem of a book – a cathartic exploration of the author's own pained childlessness, elevated by his insistent honesty, curiosity, and endearingly grumpy humor.

Jager interweaves his personal story with conversations with other childless men, hearing their compensatory strategies, seeking to formulate his own – to make his peace, as he puts it, with an unjust sentence. The irony, of course, is that the childless man so ruthlessly self-exposed here would plainly have made a caring, empathetic, if probably overprotective parent. "But closure of that nature is not in the cards," he writes sorrowfully, before characteristically bucking up and adding, "Closure, anyway, may be elusive and overrated." For those like the author who have no children, this work offers resonant insight, hope, and comfort. For those who do, it is a revelation.

David Horovitz, Editor, *The Times of Israel*

Jager has created a new genre of storytelling. Masterfully weaving together autobiography, genealogy, demography, politics, Bible stories, and interviews, he explores the cultural meanings of fatherlessness and childlessness in the notably pro-family context of modern Judaism. With fitting skepticism and good humor, Jager shakes his fist at God until he discovers in himself the enduring human qualities of compassion, acceptance, forgiveness, and gratitude.

Liberty Barnes, author of *Conceiving Masculinity: Male Infertility, Medicine, and Identity*

I loved listening to all the men in this book talk! Elliot Jager is a great storyteller and has written a daring and very personal book on an important subject we rarely get to hear about: Jewish male childlessness. Bravo!

Naomi Danis, Managing Editor, *Lilith*

Elliot Jager has written an unusual book that combines a great deal of objective information on the subjects of infertility, childlessness, and the Jewish attitude toward them, together with a very sensitive and candid personal story of his own life and inner struggle. He speaks to the reader directly, in his own distinctive voice, and brings the subject sharply into focus in a way that is both engaging and challenging. It is well worth reading.

Rabbi Reuven Hammer, author of *Akiva: Life, Legend, Legacy*

Elliot Jager

THE PATER

MY FATHER, MY JUDAISM,
MY CHILDLESSNESS

The Toby Press

The Pater
My Father, My Judaism, My Childlessness

First Edition, 2015

The Toby Press LLC
POB 8531, New Milford, CT 06776–8531, USA
& POB 2455, London W1A 5WY, England
www.tobypress.com

ISBN 978-1-59264-372-1 *hardcover*

A CIP catalogue record for this title is available from the British Library

Printed and bound in the United States

For Lisa

עֵזֶר כְּנֶגְדּוֹ

Contents

The only way to forget is to remember.
Sigmund Freud

Prologue
"Only"

This book is a personal and spiritual journey. It's about my relationship with my father and mother, my relationship with my Father "Who Art in Heaven," and it's about the meaning of life without children.

I was eight years old, sitting at the head of the table, leading the Passover Seder, surrounded by my mother, grandmother, and several elderly Lower East Side ladies, when I realized that I was not a typical kid. I was my mother's only child, and she was her mother's only child. And my father had called it quits.

The prejudices against only children, and especially against only children raised in single-parent households, are legion. Sigmund Freud posited that some of us are prone to sexual identity problems and unresolved Oedipus or Electra complexes. We're supposedly perfectionists, though I've always believed that if a job is worth doing, it may be worth doing poorly. People presume we've been over-indulged, making us self-centered. There's certainly some truth there.

Being an "only" raised by a selfless mother in a fatherless home in the 1960s meant that I had no competition for attention, food, or toys. It did, however, make it tricky for me to break the bonds of emotional dependency. My mother's moods affected me disproportionately. A perceived affront to her was just as much a slap in my face. It pained me to see her hurt. When my first marriage ran into trouble, it didn't help that the relationship between Mom and my ex had often been strained.

I felt that my mother deserved the same devotion she bestowed on me. We were co-dependents. I was her world. And she was easily the most influential person in mine. As I got older, and she became prematurely frail, I stayed close by. If I could have broken those bonds earlier without hurting her – and myself – I would have. But that would have been too painful. I derived incredible comfort from knowing she was all right. She's been dead seventeen years, yet not a day goes by that I don't feel her absence.

All this emotional baggage left me plenty neurotic. People easily confused and disappointed me. Even today I still "get my knickers in a twist" when I come up against phoniness, perfidy, or haughtiness. I used to nurse grudges more than was good for me. Fairly or not, I attribute my *meshugas*, this oversensitivity, to growing up fatherless. I assumed, I guess, that my neuroses would somehow work themselves out by raising my own children in a normal two-parent, two-child, one-dog home. And I might have succeeded, more or less, maybe – except for one small glitch: I can't have children.[1]

---

1. My friend Prof. George Mandel, formerly David Hyman Fellow in Modern Jewish Studies of the Oxford Centre for Hebrew and Jewish Studies, tells me: "The notion that having children might help parents to cure themselves of something or other is, in a way, close to what Heinrich Heine (1797–1856), the German Jewish poet, attributes to God in the poem 'Songs of Creation.' Heine portrays God as having created the world in order to cure His own sickness: 'I will gladly confess why I actually created the world: I felt the call burning in my soul like the flames of madness. Sickness was really the ultimate reason for the whole creative impulse; by creating I was able to recover, by creating I got well'" (translated by Prof. Peter Branscombe, 1967).

My chosen, if troubled, guru, the late M. Scott Peck, used to preach that emotional and spiritual health were connected – that the words are practically interchangeable. So here I am, then, one big tangle – an only child, abandoned by my Holocaust-survivor father when I was eight, raised by a self-sacrificing mother, now a childless married man, and a committed Jew.

I wrote this book as part of a process of facing up to my childlessness and its spiritual consequences. I'm a private person, so this required chucking out some of my inhibitions. At the same time, it presented the possibility of a cathartic dialogue with other childless men. I wondered what – beyond the fact of our childlessness – we might have in common. In other words, I wanted some point of personal, spiritual, and emotional comparison. I didn't want this exploration to be exclusively about myself. I wondered how my amorphous and changeable feelings jibed with those of other men. Would meeting them help me better contextualize my own situation?

So I put out the word – discreetly and only to people whose good judgment I trusted – that I was searching for childless men to interview, ideally those who'd been in relationships of one kind or another. My intermediaries would have to leave their comfort zones – the topic of childlessness is not one that typically comes up in conversation – to help me find interview subjects. There would be a huge element of triangular trust involved between myself, the intermediaries, and the interviewees. My goal was to let them tell their stories, in their own way, without injecting too much of myself into their narratives.

Like some kind of metaphysical fog, the reality of my childlessness lightly blankets my soul. On a sunny day it gets burned off by life's routine. It doesn't hang oppressively, incessantly, unremittingly over my being.

And yet it changes everything.

Chapter 1

The Pater

Every Friday afternoon at precisely 2:30 p.m., from Jerusalem, I call my 90-year-old father in Benei Berak, a largely ultra-Orthodox town adjoining Tel Aviv. We speak in Yiddish – or rather, I shout into his deaf ears. In recent years, mercifully, the Pater – as I call him on the sly, borrowing from the 1981 British television serial *Brideshead Revisited* – has become mildly tolerant of small talk. Has the grocer's delivery arrived? I ask. Or, he might volunteer – muddling the numbers – his blood pressure results taken by the visiting nurse. He might even, if prompted, fill me in on his wife's ingrown toenails. Any substantive communication, however, necessarily revolves around religious topics such as the *parasha*, the weekly Torah reading. He entreats me to recite the Book of Psalms faithfully and to observe the Sabbath fastidiously.

Reflexively, the Pater turns our Friday conversations to my being childless and invariably recommends that I seek out one or another miracle-making holy man. He collects names and brochures complete with toll-free numbers and bank deposit details. He scoffs when I tell him that Lisa and I have been to doctors, and there is nothing to be done. It's his absolute conviction that only divine intercession, mediated by a well-connected cleric, will make it possible for us to produce a man-child even now.

The Pater knows that the biblical patriarchs and matriarchs, Abraham and Sarah, Isaac and Rebecca, and Jacob and Rachel were all blessed with sons only late in life. I say that, unlike him, I am not a Hasid; that I'm a *Mitnaged* (opponent of Hasidism) and do not seek the intervention of a wonder-worker. I tell him my own prayers will have to suffice. This is a line he can get his head around even if he disagrees. It stretches the truth about my faith, but it's what I think he can handle.

My father's compulsive preoccupation with my childlessness is all the more ironic because when I was a child he abandoned me – twice. After he went away for the second time, I didn't see or speak to him for thirty years. And when I thought about him, if I thought about him at all, it was mostly with smoldering resentment. Now, the process of our halting reconciliation, which is in a race against time, is overshadowed by his unwanted, intrusive labors to move Heaven so that my sentence of childlessness will be lifted.

I wish we could talk about other things. Maybe like how much he thought about me after he left New York. In the 1960s, a boy growing up in a single-parent home was an anomaly in our strictly Orthodox milieu. In fact, it was remarkable in America at large, where only 11 percent of children in the US lived apart from their fathers, according to the Pew Research Group.[1] At the Sassover Rebbe's Eighth Street *stiebel*, the Lower East Side storefront synagogue I attended, I felt conspicuous as I tried to navigate the *davening* (prayer services) on my own. And on the High Holy Days, someone else's father – usually Shaya Kamenetsky – pulled me under his *tallit*, along with his son,

---

1. Gretchen Livingston and Kim Parker, "A Tale of Two Fathers: More Are Active, but More Are Absent," June 15, 2011, http://www.pewsocialtrends. org/2011/06/15/a-tale-of-two-fathers/.

Avrumi, shielding us with his prayer shawl from the mystical rays emanating from the *kohen*, Mr. Kraslow, whose hands were raised in the priestly blessing.

I didn't much miss my father, but his absence was more than just a nuisance. There was that Friday when I was in ninth grade at Mesiftha Tiffereth Jerusalem, and Rabbi Wasserman, the one religious studies teacher in the school I ever liked – and, now that I think about it, himself childless – offhandedly instructed us to bring a "note from your father" when we returned on Sunday certifying that we had profitably redacted a passage in the Talmud over Shabbos. Well, that sent me into a tizzy. At age fourteen, I didn't realize that Rabbi Wasserman probably already knew that my father was out of the picture; and I was too self-conscious to tell him that I didn't have a father to write a note for me.

Plainly, my mother was in no position to do it, though she came up with a suggestion: that we get one from Rabbi Usher Halpern, known in Yiddish as the *Dembeker Ruf*, a humane Old World clergyman who was on a sort of retainer to my mother's extended family. While she had tea with Rebbetzin Halpern, I took a blind stab at the talmudic passage with the *Dembeker*, who, when the Sabbath went out, kindheartedly wrote the requisite note for Rabbi Wasserman.

The Pater's disappearance also left my mother and me without money in a moribund Jewish neighborhood that was increasingly coming under violent, anti-Semitic siege – or so we felt – by Puerto Ricans and Blacks. Over time, the Sassover *stiebel*, and later the large Shneer Synagogue, a pink Moorish structure on Madison and Montgomery streets, were among any number of East Side synagogues fire-bombed, torched, or vandalized.[2] Jewish youngsters were routinely harassed. Jewish elderly were mugged with a vengeance. Unlike middle-class Jews who had made better lives for themselves in the suburbs or in more upscale sections within the five boroughs, we poor and working-class Jews were left behind to rub shoulders with New York City's burgeoning underclass, sharing tenements and housing projects.

---

2. "Synagogue Fire-Bombed On the Lower East Side; Gasoline Spilled Near Door," *The New York Times*, July 22, 1973.

This was my Lower East Side, bounded by the FDR Drive on the east, First Avenue on the west, 14th Street on the north and the Williamsburg Bridge on the south. How I envied my buddies who lived on the better side of the Williamsburg Bridge in the enclave of lower-middle-class "co-ops," constructed by the International Ladies Garment Workers Union, along Grand Street and East Broadway.

Still, I was a fairly popular kid and I managed to have my share of fun growing up. In elementary school, I always made the Chasam Sofer schoolyard punch ball team. At home, my mother catered to me – a finicky, furtively anxious child. The regulars at Sassover kind of adopted me. The Rebbe's son, Shulem Luzer Rubin, though a few years my senior, was my shul buddy. Jack and Morris Schechter, two bachelor brothers whose waning tin and roofing business stood forlornly across from the *stiebel*, would push plates of the rebbetzin's gefilte fish and *arbis* (chickpeas) my way during *shalosh seudos*, the ritual meal that marks the end of the Sabbath. There was also plenty of Ballantine Ale on offer, had I been able to stomach it.

The longer the Pater was gone, the more adept I became at airbrushing him out of my life story. No wonder my school and shul chums assumed that my father was dead. It must have struck them as peculiar, though, that I never recited *Kaddish* or the *Yizkor* memorial prayer.

But I can't airbrush out my childlessness.

Chapter 2

In Vitro, If You Can

Children had not really been on the agenda during my brief first marriage. For many years afterwards, to the extent that I even allowed myself to dream about a better future, I was hoping more for an enduring, loving relationship than for marriage and a baby carriage. But meeting Lisa in Israel was the best thing that happened to me. So the idea of creating a family with her didn't terrify me; whatever my neuroses were, they were not going to dominate my life. We were mature, level-headed, conscientious adults. Given my history, I approached the idea of kids as an awesome responsibility, but one that we were ready for.

Yet three years into our marriage, we were not getting pregnant.

Lisa was in her late thirties, so maybe age was a contributing factor. Tests showed I had poor sperm motility. Still, hadn't doctors time and again overcome just such hurdles? And so, with composed optimism, we began treatment – breaking away from our respective offices to keep appointments at Jerusalem's Hadassah Medical Center

IVF clinic on Mount Scopus.[1] We started out hopefully enough with the standard medical and social intake assessments. Next came exams, lab tests, ultrasonography, and referrals to outside consultants, including endocrinologists and urologists.

Lisa had to take potent hormonal drugs and undergo repeated surgical procedures, which necessitated mild anesthesia, to re-implant her eggs, which had been fertilized by my sperm in a test tube. My role was simply to relive the inglorious moments of my adolescence, girlie magazine in hand – only this time under doctor's orders. But the eggs that were fertilized in the lab and inserted into Lisa's uterus didn't take hold, for reasons that never became quite clear. Was it just bad luck? Were Lisa's eggs too frail? Did my sperm have a built-in self-destruct mechanism?

I couldn't help thinking back to my years at the New York City Health Department, where one of my jobs had involved working with a device that utilized a radioactive particle to detect lead in the homes of children diagnosed with lead poisoning. Employees had been repeatedly assured the machine was safe. Still, I wondered.

After each failed round, we'd return to the oval waiting room, modern, sun-drenched, with smiling baby pictures on the wall and physicians' offices around the perimeter. We'd occasionally be taken aback to see someone we knew, though the effect was more a sense of camaraderie than embarrassment. We now see some of these same women around our neighborhood, children in tow.

Our travails at Hadassah coincided with the second intifada (2000–2005), during which Palestinian terrorism, most notoriously in the form of café and bus suicide bombings, claimed over a thousand Israeli dead and six thousand wounded. Yet in the surreal cocoon of Hadassah's east Jerusalem IVF clinic we might, on any given day, be assigned to an Arab physician who was treating us with professionalism and empathy, even as, next door, a Jewish doctor might be working likewise with an Arab couple. And, save for incidental

---

1. People imagine in vitro fertilization or IVF has been around forever. Actually, the first "test tube baby" was born in 1978 thanks to the pioneering work of Professor Sir Robert Edward and Dr. Patrick Steptoe in Britain.

expenses, it didn't cost any of us a penny – or in Israeli currency, an *agora*, because all citizens and permanent residents of metropolitan Jerusalem – Jews, Arabs, Christians, and Muslims – are eligible for fertility treatment, gratis.

As a matter of national policy, little Israel is the country most committed to IVF. Just how deep-rooted this obligation is becomes apparent when you consider what happened in the early 2000s when it was challenged by the Finance Ministry on budgetary grounds.[2] In Knesset (parliamentary) hearings on the Treasury's proposal to cut the budget for IVF, Finance Ministry civil servants told lawmakers that there had been a 54 percent increase in IVF spending from 2000 to 2009. The tab was covered in the basic "health basket" – meaning that IVF was treated like a flu shot or blood pressure medicine: if you needed it, you got it. Reproduction assistance covered diagnosis and therapy for both couples and non-married childless women.

The mandarins at Finance tried to frame the discussion about IVF in straightforward public policy terms: There were limited resources; IVF was an indulgence; plainly it mustn't be allowed to take precedence over, say, cancer treatment or geriatric rehabilitation facilities. Proponents of universal free IVF came back with what amounted to a national security counter-argument. Making babies was a strategic need. Israel was a small country, demographically outnumbered, and surrounded by intractable enemies. Jews needed to remain the decided majority between the Jordan River and the Mediterranean Sea in order for the polity to remain both Jewish and democratic. The claim was put forth that it was less expensive to make babies at home than pay for mass immigration from the Diaspora.

Tellingly, pragmatic arguments about balance sheets and demographic interests didn't sway the Knesset members. What seemed to make the difference in Israel's inimitable sociocultural milieu was the emotional argument, which came from across the political spectrum. From Palestinian Arab nationalists like Ahmed Tibi (who, not

---

2. The Hebrew University of Jerusalem's Sigal Gooldin, who specializes in the sociology and anthropology of medicine, explained the debate in the April 2013 issue of the *Journal of Social Science and Medicine*.

incidentally, is a Hebrew University-trained gynecologist), to non-Zionist ultra-Orthodox MKs (Members of the Knesset), to Zionist security hawks, to dovish liberals – all coalesced behind the idea that Israeli citizens have an intrinsic "right" to parenthood, viewing infertility as a treatable ailment and IVF not only as a cure, but as a citizen's entitlement.

Men and women struggling to become parents testified before the Knesset during committee hearings, invoking this "right" to build a family. Paraphrasing the famous talmudic dictum (Nedarim 64b), one MK from the ultra-Orthodox Sephardi Shas Party declared, "If you don't have children you are as good as dead." He spoke of the angst experienced by childless couples: "Everything is extinguished. There's no happiness, just sadness."

A fertility expert testified in no less poignant terms, describing the "disease" of infertility as "no less fatal than cancer," and painting the psyches of those affected this way: "The woman is ostracized, the man cannot be part of the community, and the family ceases to exist." The recurring theme articulated by lawmakers, witnesses, and experts from disparate backgrounds was that family had a singular place in Israeli society – in both the Jewish and Arab communities.

And the most important element of family is children.

In the words of one MK: "Who among us can say that he would forgo a child? No one!" In fact, went the argument, no one should be expected to "make do" with only one child. A dovish MK said that talk of demography was beside the point. All that really mattered was "the uncomplicated need that society has to provide for couples who want to have more than one child." A rabbi-physician told a hearing: "We are dealing here with the creation of human life, and with the issue of realizing the right to parenthood. This is a basic right."

The Finance Ministry lost the budget battle and money was removed from elsewhere in the social welfare budget to protect the special place of IVF. By 2012, this "basic right" was extended to same-sex couples.

Each new day brings further advances in IVF technology, yet it's hardly the case that IVF guarantees success. All things being equal – age, health, physician skills – most women in their thirties and forties *don't* get pregnant. In our age bracket the success rate is about 20 percent. In Israel, taken as a whole, the IVF failure rate is a staggering 75 percent. These failures are attributed 30 percent of the time to women and men equally, to both jointly in 18 percent of the cases, and to no known reason 21 percent of the time. There are no empty picture frames in IVF clinic waiting rooms for all the babies that didn't get made.[3]

After five or six grueling rounds – each cycle takes about six weeks not counting waiting in between – Lisa and I decided we'd had enough. On top of everything else, we worried about the long-term consequences of the hormones she was taking. Thus, we became part of the dismal statistic: some 30 percent of infertility cases worldwide go unexplained.

Not long ago, former British Labour Party figure David Miliband described his IVF experience as "drawn out," "difficult," and "emotionally exhausting." There came a point when the Milibands too realized they "had reached the end of the line and we weren't going to give birth." They ultimately opted to go through the "daunting" process of adoption in the US and are now the parents of two young children. (David Miliband currently heads the US-based International Rescue Committee.) Although David and Louise Miliband are at least ten years younger than us, and maybe a little better connected, the question remains: Why didn't Lisa and I consider other avenues, like adoption or surrogacy?[4]

All I know is that, like the Milibands, we were emotionally drained and frustrated; we were also angry about our fate. Adoption isn't an easy process, especially not in Israel, and it would have required a resilience we just didn't have at the time. Given our ages, we

---

3. See, for instance, "Number of IVF births in Israel rises in last decade," *Jerusalem Post*, April 20, 2012; and "Over 4 percent of all babies born in Israel are conceived through IVF," *Jerusalem Post*, June 8, 2014: "One-quarter of in vitro fertilization ('test-tube baby') treatments result in a pregnancy and one-fifth in a live baby," writes Judy Siegel-Itzkovich. See, too, "Pregnant in Medical School," *The New York Times*, March 2, 2013, on unexplained infertility.

4. Surrogacy raises far more complicated issues in Jewish law than IVF, as we'll see further on. Suffice it to say that surrogacy has been legal, though hardly commonplace, in Israel since the mid-1990s.

were probably not prime candidates for a healthy local baby. Adopting from abroad would have entailed battling bureaucracies – foreign as well as Israel's own formidable officialdom. And it would not have been cheap, though that was not the deciding factor.

Moreover, I told myself that I wasn't interested in a trophy child – which was how I imagined one that wasn't our biological offspring. And anyway, adoption or surrogacy would not have changed the fact that I was the last of my line on my mother's side. The only child of an only child. The decision may appear short-sighted, but that's how I felt. Since neither Lisa nor I were ardently *for* adoption or surrogacy, we let those possibilities slide.

A friend once asked if we went through something like Elisabeth Kubler-Ross's neat five stages of grief: denial, anger, bargaining, depression, and acceptance. Real life isn't that straightforward. I felt anger, that's for sure. Especially when I read about children abused, abandoned, even murdered by their parents. Why would God give children to people who didn't want them or couldn't care for them, instead of to us?

To the extent that we are at peace with our childlessness and our decision not to adopt – it is thanks to a remarkable, humane, empathetic couples' psychologist named Edna Dolan. Edna came recommended by a close friend, and for a good number of months, first as we wound down IVF and then as we mourned the loss of the child we would never have, she became our emotional life-raft. Lisa and I usually met with Edna in her Mevaseret Zion home-office, located on a steep hilltop just outside Jerusalem. Israeli-born, Edna's excellent English came in handy, since we were not about to deal with these issues in anything but our native tongue.

We hashed out our raw feelings about a lot of things, including adoption. We did a lot of crying. Edna was our safe haven at a time when everything seemed fraught and precarious. She taught us how to listen to each other using a technique called mirroring. Sometimes I'd hear Lisa say something, but in a cognitive process of which I was only semi-aware, I'd reinterpret her feelings to fit my own preconceived notions. So to make sure lines of communication were truly open between Lisa and me, Edna showed us how to mirror, listening methodically and then prefixing our replies with, "I hear you saying that…". It may sound banal, but allowing ourselves to be clear about our feelings helped us secure and strengthen our relationship against the ravages of failed IVF treatments.

When I decided to write about Edna, I wanted to check the appropriateness of it with her first. I soon discovered the sad news that she had died of cancer some years ago. That hit me. We had last seen her when we paid a *shiva* (condolence) visit after Edna's teen-age son died in tragic circumstances. It took me weeks to find the right moment to tell Lisa that Edna herself was now gone. May her memory be a blessing.

As for why Lisa and I did not try surrogacy, that would have been even more problematic than adoption. I understand that some folks pay over $100,000 to make babies using someone else's egg, someone else's womb, and someone else's sperm. It might be right for some couples, but we weren't enthusiastic about the idea of leasing a womb – or more – from another human being, possibly in some underdeveloped country. It would have forced us to wrestle with legal, ethical, and halakhic questions at a time when our emotional stamina was low.[5] It was also true that while we knew people who'd adopted or gone through the IVF process, we just didn't know anyone who had gone the surrogacy route.

Lisa and I know any number of women who long to get married and have children, but simply have not found the right partner. Some of our friends, men and women, find the sting of loneliness less painful than the possibility of hurt that necessarily comes with attempting an intimate relationship. Of course I'm glad for the women in our circle, mostly Lisa's friends from before we were married, who had the spunk to go through IVF and bring children into this world on their own. It fascinates me that their children are growing up without dads, and I wonder if they feel "fatherless" despite never having lost one to death, divorce, or abandonment.

---

5. Rabbi David Golinkin, "What Does Jewish Law Have to Say About Surrogacy?" *Responsa*, Schechter Institute, December 2012.

Meanwhile, I can't help but think what-might-have-been thoughts as I observe children around us throwing age-appropriate tantrums, taking on likeable personas, cracking jokes, and gradually reaching bar or bat mitzva age. On such occasions, even as I take joy in the happiness of my friends and relatives, I would be dishonest to deny a sense of melancholy that Lisa and I can only be spectators to such milestones.

Not being a parent has attuned me to the various hues of childlessness.

After our failed IVF experience I made a (for me) monumental decision – though at the time I didn't admit a connection because, really, it was the culmination of a number of factors.

I took off my *kipa*.

Frum – religiously observant – from birth, I wore a yarmulke on the tough streets of the Lower East Side in the '60s and '70s, mostly without thought or choice, though sometimes defiantly in the face of abuse and bullying from my Puerto Rican neighbors. I continued to wear it for the twenty-three years I worked in New York City government. I attended meetings on behalf of my agency in some of New York's worst neighborhoods, wearing my yarmulke.

It was a decision that had been percolating for some time. Theologically, I no longer believed myself to be Orthodox, and worried I was putting up a false front. And in Israel, what one wears or doesn't wear on one's head is laden with political, religious, and cultural connotations. At the time, however, I didn't admit to myself – much less to anyone else – that there was a deeper impetus for the decision, and it wasn't just a desire to avoid phoniness.

The first few days, it was awkward to go bareheaded. At work, several people asked me what was going on. None got a straight answer because I didn't have one. Instead, I resorted to my lifelong fallback: I made a joke and changed the subject. But the truth was I felt let down by the Creator of the Universe and I needed to let Him know. I felt God had hidden His face from me, and keeping my *kipa* in my pocket was a form of personal protest. It was also a belated rebellion against my spiritually wasted yeshiva years. And it was my own silent stand against those who defame God's holy name by behaving badly with little thought to the yarmulkes on their heads.

At first, my decision left me uneasy. In the Diaspora, yarmulkes are partly intended to declare membership in the tribe, to identify Jews among gentiles. In Israel, they are more like bumper stickers. Jewish Israeli men are defined not only by whether they wear a *kipa*, but by its style – velvet, large, and black for the ultra-Orthodox, knitted for the national-religious, and endless variations in between.

In post-biblical times, Jewish custom demanded men and (married) women cover their hair: women for the sake of modesty, both sexes as a sign of God above. A mid-nineteenth century code of Jewish conduct and law held that "a man ought not to walk four cubits" bareheaded because doing so "suggests overbearing pride, ignoring God's omnipresence."[6] By the seventeenth century, Jews made a point of covering their heads in contradistinction to Christians, who even prayed bareheaded.

I had never explicitly tied the decision to stop wearing a *kipa* to my childlessness – to feeling abandoned by my Father in Heaven. In hindsight, though, it seems as if it was integral. Much later I told my friend George about my *kipa* saga, and he said that whenever he hears that some great personal misfortune has led X to change his view of life, or of God – "and I definitely include myself in this, and I speak from my own experience" – he wonders whether the evidence was there all along but X ignored it, or its implications, until the misfortune happened to him personally.

Addressing himself to my case, George said: "You must have known long before you met Lisa that there were childless people who longed for children and would have made good parents, but that knowledge didn't have much effect, if any, on your attitude to God. The fact that He had let other people down didn't make much impression on you. That is, in a sense, quite obvious and understandable;

---

6. It is not clear that during talmudic times people covered their heads. In modern times, certain Orthodox halakhic authorities have permitted men to go to work bareheaded when circumstances require it.

but once you start to think about it, it raises questions about us and our capacity for fellow-feeling."

I can't disagree.

Dan Lobel,[7] whom I knew from my days as a technical writer at a high-tech firm in Tel Aviv, is one of those lanky, earnest, analytical people who don't make you feel uncomfortable for not sharing their spiritual passions. I joke that he'd make a good Jewish Dalai Lama. He's principled, ascetic, and always seems to stay on an even keel. Like me and Lisa, he and his wife Tzipi tried IVF only to find it did not work for them.

Born in Toronto, Dan was already in his thirties when he embarked on a two-year trek, mostly in Asia, in search of some greater purpose to his life. His parents were non-practicing Reform Jews who only rarely attended Temple. They perfunctorily sent him to Sunday school, where his interest in Judaism remained, unsurprisingly, dormant.

"I was on a shoestring budget when I arrived in Jerusalem in the autumn of 1995. Costs were considerably more than what I had become accustomed to in Asia. So, I started working as a night check-in clerk at a hostel," Dan recalls. "I was meeting all sorts of travelers who were saying things like, 'Isn't Jerusalem awesome and spiritual?' and it just wasn't clicking with me. I was in a funk, sleeping during the day, getting up at 5 p.m. for 'breakfast' just as the sun was going down, and spending my nights folding guests' laundry, emptying ashtrays and cleaning toilets. I was considering moving on when my travel buddy suggested I do a class. He said that Aish HaTorah, in Jerusalem's Old City, was running a seminar. So I took off a few nights from work and went." Dan enrolled first in Aish HaTorah and later at Ohr Somayach, two academies which specialize in *kiruv*, making Orthodox Judaism accessible to unaffiliated young Jews, most of whom do not stay on in Israel.

---

7. It takes a lot of courage to talk about a sensitive subject, especially for the first time and to a stranger. To protect the privacy of men without children whom I interviewed for this book, I changed their names, disguised certain non-germane autobiographical details and, sometimes, the precise circumstances of our dialogue.

"I recall signs directing participants to the Aish building – things were more Spartan than today – with the word 'Discovery' and arrows pointing you through the maze of Jerusalem's Old City. And below the arrows was the catchphrase: 'If you have questions….' I recall thinking to myself, 'Questions? What questions? I don't have any questions.' God was completely off my radar at that point. But the program turned out to be fascinating, touching on religion, history, philosophy, science. Although I had no questions going in, I came out with a whole pile of them." Dan studied three months at Aish and another three at Ohr Somayach. By the time he returned to Canada he was on an Orthodox trajectory.

He eventually found his way back to Israel where, at a Shabbat luncheon, he met another English speaker, an attractive, tender-hearted social worker with a porcelain complexion named Tzipi. The chemistry was just right.

As I sat speaking with Dan in their living room, he told me about their journey through infertility treatments. Within two years of their marriage, seeing they weren't getting pregnant, the couple began IVF at Jerusalem's Hadassah Hospital on Mount Scopus – the same place Lisa and I had undergone our treatments. They told almost no one. He was 44 and she was 37.

It turns out that Tzipi has an unbearable fear of needles, and the IVF process requires that you inject yourself at the same time every day with hormones. She tried it for a while, but just couldn't do it herself. So Dan would go to her workplace to give her the jab. "There we were in the storage room among grimy documents, decaying newspapers, and stale, empty beer bottles. Me with the syringe in my hands, Tzipi often bursting into tears. Finally, she just completely dissolved. She couldn't carry on. I can't say I was surprised. When Tzipi goes for an immunization, she practically passes out."

Dan's story reminded me of how Lisa would sometimes show up at *The Jerusalem Post*, when I was an editor there, for her jab. We'd lock ourselves in the dusty newspaper morgue for the procedure. We, however, came out smiling – God only knows what my colleagues surmised.

Dan told me he was angry – at Tzipi, at himself, at the situation – for something like twenty-four hours. "Then I said to myself, 'OK. It hurts. And I wish we could do something about that. But nothing hurts me more than seeing Tzipi hurting.'" Afterwards, he told me, "I just decided everyone has their limits about certain things, and what's the point of being angry? She had reached her limit – there was no doubt.

"People think IVF is as simple as popping an aspirin," Dan added. "They don't have problems having children, and only become aware of those who do when they hear about a successful IVF outcome. Most people going through IVF don't broadcast it. So if they are unsuccessful, no one will ever know; outsiders will never get a sense of the percentage of failures vis-à-vis successes.

"People whom IVF has failed, for one reason or another, are not flag-wavers. I'm in that 75 percent."

Barely catching their breath after their IVF ordeal, Dan and Tzipi decided to adopt a child. "We went through all the hoops. All the meetings, interviews, paperwork, psychological evaluations, a day-long psychometric exam, for which we paid NIS 2,500 ($680). There was a hilarious interview with a psychologist who was evaluating our answers and showing us, I swear to you, Rorschach blots, asking us what we saw; it was like out of a movie. I couldn't believe people still did that.

"So we went through all of that. And the last phase for getting approved for adoption is that they come for a visit to make sure you don't live in filth, with rats. The social worker came to our home and saw that we were clean and normal. She told us that everything was good to go: 'You guys should have no problem getting accepted.'"

Because of their ages, they were not eligible to adopt a healthy newborn, though they could adopt a child between ages six and ten who most likely would come with some disadvantage or impairment. Dan had concerns about the undertaking, but was willing to go ahead anyway. Now, it was just a matter of getting written confirmation in the mail after the adoption approval committee had made its formal decision. Weeks stretched into months and still Dan and Tzipi heard nothing.

Then, out of the blue, came an awful blow. Dan became aware of a growth, and his worst fears were realized when the biopsy results came back positive. A random unexpected occurrence had fundamentally changed Dan's life. He went from prospective new dad to cancer patient.

"We were on the cusp of adoption, and God said no.

"About two weeks into dealing with the cancer horror, we got a call from the social worker asking if we were coming to the parenting class. It's the class you have to go through once you've been approved. And then you can adopt.

"And we said, 'Approved?'

"'Didn't you get the letter?'

"'No.'"

They never did get the letter of approval. And because of Dan's cancer treatment, they couldn't attend the class.

Although Dan is now in remission, he still hasn't regained his full stamina, and he and Tzipi are no longer sure the conventional adoption program they were involved in makes sense for them. They are exploring becoming emergency foster parents – "for when the cops have to pull a child out of the house at 3 a.m. – the catch being you have to be willing to care for three children at a time, under the age of six, who are all coming from trauma," Dan explains.

Still another program they're considering would allow them to adopt the newborn baby of a drug addict. The catch is that such an infant would essentially go through withdrawal, and may need detoxification. By signing up for the program Dan and Tzipi would be on a fast track to becoming the infant's permanent adoptive parents. The downside is that such a child may well be damaged by their prenatal exposure to narcotics, and there is no guarantee Dan and Tzipi would be approved to officially adopt the infant. They might care for it for six months or more while its legal status is clarified, only to be told they must give up the child.

It's not a frivolous decision, and they're waiting until Dan feels more like himself before making the final call.

I asked him what he tells people when they casually ask if he has children. He said his stock answer is, "No, *be'ezrat Hashem* – God willing." When I raised an eyebrow, he replied, "Look, Tzipi hasn't gone through menopause. We're still in the game. A miracle can happen. Why not?"

Of course, I said, there are all these folks who purposefully opt not to have kids. They wonder about the wisdom of bringing children into the world. Some worry that they won't be good parents. Some had such traumatically lousy childhoods that they can't imagine having the inner resources to give a child what he or she needs. Dan reserved judgment. "There is more than selfishness to consider. There are people who think the world is such a mess, they don't want to bring kids into it."

Dan and I agreed that this stance is somehow un-Jewish. However, Dan then surprised me by asking, "But what makes it 'un-Jewish' in your eyes?" My reply was knee-jerk. It is "un-Jewish" because Jews are part of a collective, and in order to have quality, we also need quantity. "That's like a fascist view of Judaism," Dan countered. "That everything is done for the nation."

I recoiled at the fascist accusation. Had I the presence of mind, I might have quoted Emil Fackenheim's proposition about not giving Hitler any posthumous victories. We need to make lots of babies *auftzuluchis* – to spite Hitler – just to dance on his grave. Not seeing my Judaism through Dan's religious lens – or at least not with his sense of certainty and profound faith – for me being Jewish is, indeed, foremost a notion of peoplehood.

"Stating that by choosing not to have kids you're not contributing to the gene pool – to me, that's a very non-Jewish approach. Or, at least, not a specifically Jewish approach," Dan added. Dan's point is that procreation is the first imperative for *all* of humanity, and not exclusive to Judaism.

"All right, then what makes it un-Jewish not to have kids, in your eyes?" I asked.

"I think a very Jewish approach to life is always optimism and the hope of things getting better, whether on a national level – believing in redemption and the Messiah – or, on a personal level, in growth and self-development. Judaism has put an incredibly strong emphasis on hope. Despite all the odds, despite all the tragedies, despite all the difficulties. To say 'look how terrible the world is' and to come to the decision not to have kids – that, to me, is un-Jewish. Looking at the world as a mess and saying I am not going to bring anyone into this is un-Jewish because it denies hope. It denies that things can get better, that you can play a part in their getting better. Whereas, Elliot, your answer has nothing to do with Judaism."

Chapter 3

Reconciliation

The Pater and I had arranged to meet outside the post office on Rabbi Akiva Street, a main drag in Benei Berak. I looked out for an older bearded man, and there was no shortage of them. When the right one came along, he inquired, "Elie Yaeger?" and we hastily, inelegantly shook hands.

Why, after a thirty-year-plus gap, I consented to meet the Pater during a 1994 visit to Israel is something I cannot say for sure. Curiosity was part of it, and maybe I wanted to show him that I had more than survived without him. The rendezvous, which had my mother's blessing, had been orchestrated by the Pater's sister, my Tante Golda.

Golda was the quintessential European Jewish aunt. She had been through hell – a hardscrabble upbringing, Auschwitz, tragic widowhood – and yet, somehow, she managed to smile. She lived on East Broadway above a kosher bakery in a building sandwiched between the left-leaning *Forverts* (Forward) and the right-leaning

Tante Golda: the Pater's sister and Auschwitz survivor

Der Morgen Zshurnal (Morning Journal) Yiddish newspapers. Unaffected, short, and *zaftig* (chubby), her motto was *nem zeich tze mol nicht zum hartz* – which, loosely translated, means, "Don't get upset, eat." I used to think of Golda as unconventional because for supper she would serve store-bought delicatessen. My mother never served store-bought anything when I was growing up – and certainly not delicatessen.

The Pater was no less a stranger to Golda than to me. Maybe she hoped to bond with him vicariously, through me. As if the Pater was the bonding type. Anyhow, I managed to visit Israel from time to time and Golda didn't, so the job was mine. Golda had seen my father just once since he'd left New York, years earlier during a synagogue-sponsored Israel trip. That turned out to be a fiasco, a melancholy reunion, to say the least, because their ailing older brother, Chaim Yitzhak, died. Poor Golda. On her one and only sojourn outside America since arriving as a World War II refugee, she spent that vacation sitting *shiva* with my uncommunicative Pater.

Not the worldliest of souls, Golda vaguely recollected only that the Pater lived in an ultra-Orthodox neighborhood. For contact details, she had a post office box number in Jaffa, where she'd send money before the Jewish festivals. Years later, when telephones became commonly available in Israel, the Pater conferred upon Golda his number which – never employed – she eventually passed on to me.

That is how the Pater and I came to be strolling along one late summer afternoon, both of us a bit unnerved. I glanced at the disheveled, shambling, rather defeated figure who was my father in the flesh, and found myself struck by the chasm between who he was and how I had remembered him, which was fiery and volatile. He must have been equally taken aback by me, clean-shaven, wearing a diminutive knitted *kipa* rather than the large black velvet yarmulke and black garb favored by the ultra-Orthodox.

Still, he invited me back to his cramped, squalid apartment with its shared communal toilet. There, for the first time, I met his "new" wife, Devora, and my half-sister, Esti. Back in 1991, during a previous trip, my mother and I had had tea in the lobby of a Jerusalem hotel with my other half-sister, Sheindel, and her then-new husband, Moshe Chaim, scion of an old-line Breslov family. That strange night in the hotel lobby, too, had been orchestrated at Golda's behest.

The two ex-sisters-in-law, Golda and my mother, Yvette, had grown closer over the years. Toward the end of my mother's life, in January 1997, Tante Golda had fallen in her Brighton Beach apartment, dislocating a shoulder. With her own health hanging by a thread, my mother decided to be *mevaker ḥolim*, to pay a convalescent call, to Golda. It was to be my mother's last journey from the Lower East Side before she succumbed to a massive stroke later that month.

But – talk about a small world – during that first reunion between me and the Pater, my mother was having coffee and cake nearby at the Benei Berak apartment of the father and stepmother of Rebecca Kantrowitz, an Israeli-American classmate of mine from grad school at New York University. It just so happened that they lived a few blocks away from the Pater. I took my mother there because I wanted her close by, the pretext being that she could meet Rebecca's father and stepmother while I saw the Pater. The underlying purpose was that I didn't want her to feel that I was meeting the Pater behind her back.

Nor did I inform the Pater that my mother was with me in Benai Berak.

Afterwards, I was too flummoxed to say much about the visit, though I recall describing the squalor in which the Pater and his family then lived. "But his wife and daughters were very cordial, plying me with refreshments and full of questions about my life in America," I added. I was trying to reassure my mother, I suppose, that she'd made the right decision; that had she immigrated to Israel in the late 1950s, as the Pater wanted, she could have been the one sharing a toilet with the neighbors. I didn't want her to think I was wavering in my loyalty to her.

I think my mother ultimately wanted me to pursue a relationship with the Pater, as if I could help solve the mystery that had bedeviled her: what made him tick. And, indeed, increased exposure to the Pater's opaque persona has given me an opportunity to fathom his character. Allowing for the obvious, that thirty years-plus have changed us both, it strikes me that the pious, ascetic lifestyle he so hankered after in America and now lives in Israel is driven by gnawing fears, incited by chronic nightmares, and fed by terrible fixations. My father lives with a sense of imminent doom that can only be relieved – temporarily – by superstitious rituals and dodgy religious practices. With time, I began to understand why.

He is respected in the community for his piety. His daughters revere him as a gentle *tzaddik* (righteous person) who is quicker to chuckle than to scold. Now that he is old and in frail health, Esti – who lives nearby with her husband and family – is devoted to his care. Batya and Gabriel who run the *makolet*, the grocery store, near his home, where customers customarily shop on credit, know my father as an honorable man. Batya tells me, "He's the kind of person who won't sleep at night if he doesn't pay a debt on time." A retired, white-bearded hasidic neighbor, Reb Wassertiel, who once worked with the Pater in Tel Aviv's Carmel Market, told me, unsolicited, that my father was a saintly soul and that "there are not many like him."

I've come to believe that the Pater's flight from rudimentary paternal responsibility when I was a boy, his embrace of extreme religion, his dysfunctional disinterest in day-to-day practicalities, his peculiar lack of curiosity about ordinary life beyond the utilitarian cannot – any of it – be detached from his primordial struggle to stave off the demons of his past.

The Pater was born on January 12, 1923, in the town of Spinka (*Sapanca* or *Săpânța*, Maramureș county) in northern Romania's Carpathian Mountain area, bordered by Hungary, Slovakia, and the Ukraine. As the crow flies, Spinka is probably closer to Krakow and the Poland of my mother's family than to Romania's capital, Bucharest. There were fewer than one thousand Jews in the town when he lived there, although they comprised about 23 percent of the population. My father, Anshel, and his siblings – Chaim Yitzhak, Golda, and a younger sister, Sarah, led what could only have been dreary, impoverished lives. Golda was farmed out by their stern-looking mother (a capricious judgment, I know, based on a single official photograph in my possession) to her husband's sister, Bat-Sheva, and her brother-in-law, Ephraim Moshe, who at the time had no children of their own.

The Pater told me that his father, Eliahu, uncharacteristically in those days, had married for love. "My mother was a *bat-kohen* [the daughter of a member of the priestly class], and my father was not an especially learned man. It was unusual that someone who was not a *talmid ḥakham*, a Torah scholar, would marry a woman with such *yiḥus* [pedigree]."

My grandfather and his brother, my great-uncle Wolf-Ber, married two sisters. "Two brothers marrying two sisters is not ideal, the rabbis frown upon it," the Pater told me. "But my father fell in love with her. She was pretty." The Pater's mother, my grandmother Risa, died before World War II, when he was in his late teens, from what, beyond "swollen feet," he does not know. My father had no secular education, having attended *ḥeder* (a rudimentary elementary school teaching the basics of Judaism) and later studied *Gemara* (Talmud) in a Spinka yeshiva headed by Rebbe Hershel Kahana.

During a break from reviewing the *parasha* (biblical portion) of the week, I asked the Pater what he used to do for fun. I couldn't think of the Yiddish word, so I tried the Hebrew, *kef.* He had no answer; he didn't really grasp the concept.[1] "I helped my father," was the best he could finally come up with. My grandfather koshered meat for a living after a hand injury made it impossible for him to keep his own flock of sheep. The Pater apprenticed with him, extracting veins and other animal parts in the koshering process.

Life must have been bleak. Then came Hitler.

In the course of the Second World War, half of Romania's Jews were killed by the Nazis and their enablers. My grandfather was probably worked to death someplace in Hungary or Romania. Little Sarah – who would have been in her early teens at most – died in Auschwitz.[2]

Thanks to the random kindness of a fellow inmate who worked in the camp's kitchen – yet herself didn't endure – Golda survived Auschwitz. Chaim Yitzhak must have fled Romania early in the war, finding refuge in Stalin's Russia. He, too, survived, and eventually made it to the newly reborn Jewish state, having shed religion and become an agnostic.

The Pater had been forced into a labor battalion, probably digging trenches and doing road and railway construction. Toward the end of the war he found himself first in Hungary, then in Austria; it was around Pesaḥ (Passover) time. He was determined to barter his bread allotment for potato *remlich*, both because they would last longer and so as not to eat bread, which is forbidden during the festival. My father is a born follower, which paid off when he took the advice of a savvier prisoner, and finagled a way to stay behind when his contingent was marched on – probably to their deaths.

Within days Soviet forces arrived, and Anshel was liberated. The war was over.

---

1. Actually, Israelis adopted *kef* from the Arabic. In case you're wondering, fun in Yiddish is *shpas*. To which my friend and neighbor Ruthie Rossing, a translator and Yiddishist, quips: "Shpas, huh? More or less, but the meaning is closer to 'jest' or 'joke,' or 'a kidding remark.' Yiddish speakers were never known for idly having fun."
2. I am named in Hebrew after my father's father, Eliahu. Sarah's name was perpetuated when my half-sister named a daughter after her. The names of my paternal grandmother, Risa Miriam, similarly live on.

My father, now 22, made his way to Budapest, where the American Jewish Joint Distribution Committee had set up a shelter for refugees. I think back to where I was at that age – in my penultimate year at Brooklyn College, writing an honors paper for Prof. Herbert Druks on the controversial, Hungarian-centered, Holocaust-era Joel Brand Affair – all the while ignorant of the Pater's own Shoah ordeal.

Anyhow, he then traveled back to Spinka, where, providentially, he was reunited with Golda. There was nothing else there for them: no property, and certainly no lives to rebuild. So together they headed for Bamberg, Germany, in the American Zone, and found asylum in a Displaced Persons Camp. It was in that DP camp that Golda married Naftali Einhorn, also a survivor, in a modest ceremony attended by my father; it was also where my first cousin, Risa Einhorn, was born in 1947. Naftali's father was already in America, and neither he nor my father was keen to be drafted into the nascent Israeli army. They had survived the war; they didn't want to go through another. So they sought, and in due course received, permission to enter the US as naturalized citizens.

His first official American documents show Anshel, as he was always known in the family, as clean-shaven and good-looking. He'd changed his given name from Anton to Alan, and as he set foot on American soil in 1949, to every outward appearance he seemed a man ready for a fresh start. Appearances notwithstanding, he must have been lonely and bewildered. Perhaps, in a different world, under different circumstances, my traumatized father might have embarked upon a regimen of psychological analysis, talk therapy, and self-discovery. Instead, over a lifetime, the only opiate within his grasp for grappling with anxiety, angst, and sleep disturbance has been a superstitious strain of ultra-Orthodox hasidic Judaism.

It's not that he didn't try to acculturate to the American way of life. Soon after he arrived, he found a job at Mendelowitz's butcher shop on First Avenue, helping with orders and deliveries. In a form he filled out in 1950 he listed his occupation as "dental mechanic" – warranted by a vocational training course he was taking. There followed a succession of jobs – at a sportswear store, luncheonette, Streit's Matzo Factory, another butcher shop on the West Side, a curtain store on Orchard Street, back to sportswear, then as an operator in a textile house.

Yet for all his pains, he remained a stranger in a strange land.

Chapter 4

"Why Weepest Thou?"

I f the Pater knew that Lisa and I sit next to each other, family-style, in our Conservative (Masorti) synagogue in Jerusalem, he'd be aghast. The notion that women and men should play an equal role in the service and synagogue hierarchy is anathema to his worldview – and, truth be told, is light years away from the life I once led on the Lower East Side, where the Orthodox synagogue was as much a men's club and fraternal organization as a house of study and prayer. In London, too, established Orthodoxy, worn lightly in the form of the United Synagogue, held sway when Lisa was growing up. She'd sit with her mother and two sisters, way up in the women's gallery, gossiping and praying while, down below, a decorous service was being conducted by the spiffily attired men.[1]

---

1. Modern Orthodoxy in America, Britain, and Israel invites women to assume non-liturgical leadership roles, distinguishing it from the ultra-Orthodox model familiar to me from the Lower East Side. Lisa's former United Synagogue

Liturgically, the egalitarian Conservative congregation we now attend in our Jerusalem neighborhood essentially adheres to the prevailing Orthodox rite. We use the traditional Israeli prayer books for Shabbat and holidays, making only the most minor semantic adjustments. In this way, or so goes the theory, anyone Jewishly literate walking into our *davening* would immediately recognize the service.

Like all traditional congregations, on the first day of Rosh HaShana, the Jewish New Year, we read from the Book of Samuel (1:8). The storyline goes like this: Elkanah has two wives, the fecund Peninnah and the beloved but barren Hannah, who is disconsolate over not being able to conceive. Whether out of empathy or impatience, Elkanah asks, "Why weepest thou? Am I not better to thee than ten sons?"

I'm not sure Elkanah gets it.

Hannah, broken with grief, heads to the tent sanctuary in Shiloh, dwelling place of the Ark of the Covenant, to pray. Hannah is mumbling in supplication when she's spied by the High Priest, Eli. Oddly, he misreads her demeanor as drunkenness. As soon as Hannah makes clear what's really happening, however, Eli backtracks, prophesying that she will have the son she longs for.

And so it goes in all such biblical stories. She gives birth to Samuel – though rather than taking joy in raising him with her husband, she apprentices the boy to the priests as soon as he's weaned. He grows up to become one of the greatest biblical prophets, albeit with evident anger-management issues (see, inter alia, Samuel 15:32–33).

For years, every Rosh HaShana I would sneak a glance at Lisa as the story of Hannah was intoned; she'd be stoically scanning her prayer book as though the narrative had nothing do to with us. The tension between fecundity and barrenness is a fairly constant, I'd say almost obsessive, biblical theme. Will Abraham and Sarah conceive a child? Will Isaac and Rebecca? In fact, from Genesis through Chronicles, the Hebrew Bible does not record a single instance where God turns a deaf ear to the prayers of a barren couple. Not once.

---

congregation in London tried recently to go further: when removed from the ark on the Sabbath, the Torah was passed briefly to the women's section before being returned to the men's side to be read. This experiment was soon discontinued.

Yet it is telling that there are no explicit references to male infertility in the Bible.[2] The biblical characters who bear the brunt of the angst associated with childlessness are women. Conveniently, every biblical husband of an infertile wife can demonstrate his virility and fecundity thanks to having at least one other, fertile wife in reserve.

Genesis actually offers a precursor to the Elkanah-Hannah romance in describing Jacob's enduring love for the infertile Rachel over the fabulously fruitful but unloved Leah. And still, Rachel pleads with Jacob, "Give me children, or else I die" (Gen. 30:1). Sure enough, and in the fullness of time, Rachel does give Jacob his favorite son, Joseph (number 11, if you're counting sequentially). Tragically, however, Rachel is destined to die giving birth to their second son, Benjamin.

It is all the more striking, then, that in Jewish tradition it is not Leah (and certainly neither of the concubines Bilha and Zilpa), but Rachel who is the maternal heroine, her burial place a destination for Jewish women from all over the world.

She overcame infertility – even if it killed her.[3]

Every weekday, scores of Jewish women – and men – make their way by bus or car to the heavily fortified compound where tradition teaches that Jacob buried his beloved Rachel. The site abuts Bethlehem, a town under Palestinian control since the 1993 Oslo Accords. Inside the air-conditioned shrine, the velvet-draped raised

---

2. Christian Bible scholar John Byron points out that male infertility is only implied – for instance, in the stories of Tamar and Ruth, whose first husbands left them childless though they later went on to have children.

3. By the by, there are very few examples in the Bible of women not placing children at the forefront of their preferences. Dr. George Savran, a senior lecturer in Bible at Jerusalem's Schechter Institute of Jewish Studies, calls my attention to the work of Gail Twersky Reimer. In her book of imaginative reconstruction, *Reading Ruth* (New York: Ballantine Books, 1994), Reimer suggests that Ruth does not necessarily want children. It's Naomi who has a preoccupation with them. Savran also points me to the story of Elisha and the Shunnamite woman in ii Kings 4:8–37. "Notice that she is hesitant about her desire for a child," says Savran "and critical of Elisha for assuming that she does want one. Both texts end with the birth or revival of a child, but they raise interesting questions regarding the accepted norm in the Bible about having children."

tomb is divided by a wooden partition – men on one side and women on the other. Supplicants come pleading for Rachel's intercession with the Heavenly Court for children, or more children, or more boy-children. There is an adjoining study hall for ultra-Orthodox men and there are beggars, both men and women, to complete the pilgrimage experience by accepting alms.

Time and time again, throughout the Bible, barrenness is depicted as divine punishment. Take the convoluted story of Michal, which, like the story of Hannah, also appears in the Book of Samuel. "Now Michal daughter of Saul had fallen in love with David…" (1 Sam. 18:20). It's not every day that a woman's love for a man is unambiguously documented in a biblical narrative. But there it is.

Sensing a threat to his power, Saul forces David to flee the royal court. Michal lies to her father by not admitting that she helped David escape. Next, Saul gives Michal to Paltiel, though the Talmud would have us believe that their relationship remained unconsummated. David returns to claim Michal after Saul is killed in battle – apparently because it makes good political sense given her royal lineage. Paltiel takes this turn of events badly.

As the narrative unfolds in the second book of Samuel (6:20–23), Michal sardonically criticizes David for his ecstatic dancing – or was it sexual exhibitionism – during delivery of the Ark of the Covenant from Hebron to Jerusalem. The two have a heated public spat, after which the Bible relates: "And Michal, Saul's daughter, never bore a child until the day she died."

Of course, David's other wives did.

The rabbis of the Talmud (Sanhedrin 19b) try to reinterpret the narrative. Some have her adopting her sister's children; another tradition holds out the possibility that she was able to bear children after all. Still, the message lingers: not having children is meant as some kind of divine retribution.

Throughout the centuries of Jewish civilization, making babies has always been the first imperative. The Jews are the *children* of Abraham. In the canonized Jewish texts, the Jewish people are repeatedly referred to as the *sons and daughters* of Israel. Our common destiny is as *Klal Yisrael.*[4] Membership is open. There is a process by which non-Jews can join – though different Jewish tribes disagree about the membership rules. Nevertheless, once you're in, you become part of the *family.* Judaism is a culture rooted in the Land of Israel, the covenant idea, peoplehood, polity, the Hebrew language, and, to an extent, ethnicity. It is also a religion. In *Judaism as a Civilization*, 1934, Rabbi Mordechai Kaplan (1881–1983) tried to pull all these strands together by conceptualizing Judaism as an "evolving religious civilization," wrestling with God, nationhood, and ritual in a never-ending search for meaning.

Truth be told, though, that search for meaning is made incomparably more complicated for those without children. Abraham himself confronts this dilemma when he challenges God: "What can You give me, seeing that I shall die childless?" (Gen. 15:2) And when the Jewish national condition seemed most bleak, the ancient prophets invoked childlessness as their chosen metaphor. The prophet Isaiah, for example, likened Zion's distress during the First Temple period to infertility: "Sing, O barren one, You who bore no child!" (Is. 54:1)

When there are good tidings, however, God's countenance is directly tied to the blessings of a fecund womb. The Psalmist intones, "Sons are the provision of the Lord; the fruit of the womb, *His reward*" (127:3–5).

God Himself fertilizes Mother Earth with water and rivers. He instructs and blesses humanity, created in His image, to "Be fruitful, and multiply" (Gen. 1:28).[5] God is the quintessence of creativity; He wants us to be like Him.

---

4. *"Klal Yisrael"* may be one expression of shared community and destiny among all Jews.

5. Prof. David Daube (1909–1999), the great German Jewish expert on ancient law, posited that "Be fruitful, and multiply" was actually not a command but a blessing; and indeed, the phrase is introduced with "And God blessed them, and God said unto them, 'Be fruitful, and multiply.'" Only later did Judaism begin to read this passage as a command. I am indebted to George Mandel for bringing Daube to my attention. As Mandel tells me, basing himself on Daube, "God speaks the same words to the sea monsters, the creepy-crawlies, and the winged

The Midrash in Genesis Rabba links infertility to death based on the placement of two Bible passages:[6] "Whoso sheddeth man's blood, by man shall his blood be shed; for in the image of God made He man" (Gen. 9:6), which is immediately followed by "And you, be fruitful, and multiply; swarm in the earth, and multiply therein." This teaches, according to the Midrash, that failure to bring children into the world is a form of suicide, if not murder.[7]

There's a lot of back-and-forth in the Talmud about whether the "Be fruitful and multiply" commandment falls singularly on the shoulders of the man. The Mishna in Yevamot 65b is explicit: "A man is commanded concerning the duty of propagation, but a woman is not."

Naturally, that hardly settles the matter. Talmudic discourse is dialectic – like an arrow observed flying in mid-air. The final word is elusive.[8]

It is not just the God of the Jews who places primacy on procreation. All ancient civilizations – Egyptian, Sumerian, Canaanite, Phoenician, Hittite, and Greek, among others – placed a high value on fertility.

Among non-Western civilizations, Hinduism is second to none in dreading childlessness. Maybe it's because Hindus believe that their newborn children are already connected to them through previous incarnations. Among the most traditional, sons are considered far

---

birds a few verses before He says them to human beings. Since animals don't have any mitzvot, the words can't be intended as a mitzva the first time they're spoken, so why should we suppose they're intended as a mitzva the second time?" Rashi, the authoritative French medieval commentator on Bible and Talmud, is not persuaded. He says read the text plainly: the first reference as a blessing and the second as a commandment.

6. The Midrash is an anthology of rabbinical commentaries and homiletic stories on the Torah. Genesis Rabba, circa 400 CE, is one of the oldest in the genre.

7. See Yakov Meir's column on Noah, "Of Retribution and Reproduction / *Parashat Noach*," *Haaretz*, October 4, 2013.

8. For more on the subject, I recommend a summary of a lecture by Rabbi Aharon Lichtenstein, "*Peru U-Revu*" and "*Shevet*," which the Orthodox scholar delivered at Yeshivat Har Etzion. Searchable on the Internet, it has been summarized by Yitzchak Barth and translated by David Silverberg.

more desirable than daughters. As for Hindus with no children at all, well, their lives are deemed "inauspicious."[9] Perhaps because of the overwhelming stigma attached to a marriage without children, when all else fails, increasing numbers of childless Hindu couples are even willing to adopt girls!

In the Buddhist tradition, the Buddha came as a blessing to his previously childless parents, Mahamaya and Suddhodhana.[10] That's why they named him Siddhartha, which means "every wish fulfilled." Procreation may not be a fundamental religious tenet in Buddhism, but anecdotal evidence suggests that Chinese, Thai, or Burmese Buddhists obsess just as much as anyone else about having children.

In contrast to the Hebrew Bible, the New Testament seems to have fewer barrenness and salvation plotlines.[11] There's Joachim and Anna, who are advanced in age when Mary is born. Plainly, Mary is neither elderly nor barren when she gives birth to Jesus. Instead, what matters in the Christian tradition is that Jesus' birth is to a virgin.

Incidentally, some Jewish commentators make the case that the Jewish obsession with childlessness is at least partly a post-biblical reaction to external factors – namely pagan self-mutilation rites that result in sterility, and later Catholic championing of celibacy for its clergy.

Among the major faiths, Islam seems comparatively less preoccupied with childlessness – perhaps because it is producing so many babies.[12] As distinct from Jesus' virgin birth, Islam's founder, the

---

9. For an overview of Hindu attitudes toward childlessness, see "Children and Hinduism" http://www.hinduwebsite.com/hinduism/h_children.asp. On adopting girls rather than having no children at home at all, see "Now, childless couples prefer to adopt girls," *Times of India*, Nov 23, 2012.

10. See "The Buddha: History and Legend," http://www.netplaces.com/buddhism/the-buddha-history-and-legend/siddhartha-gautama.htm.

11. There are some thirty-four references to childlessness in the Christian Bible. See "Childlessness," http://www.openbible.info/topics/childlessness.

12. Which is not to downplay the suffering of childless persons in the Muslim and Arab world (or anywhere else). My understanding is that artificial reproduction technologies receive little government financial support in poor countries like

prophet Muhammad, had a rather natural, albeit difficult, start in life given that his father, Abdallah, died before the prophet was born, and his mother, Amina, survived only until the boy was six years old.

The Koran confirms that Allah blessed Ibrahim (Abraham) and Sarah with a child late in life. The collection of Islamic teachings known as the *Hadith* includes the tale of the revolutionarily monotheistic Asiya. She's known as the wife of the nefarious – and impotent – Pharaoh, who rescues baby Moses and raises him as her own. Asiya ultimately goes to her Maker as righteous as she was childless. There is also the story of the prophet Zakariya, whose wife, Ishba, gives birth to the righteous Yahya only thanks to divine intervention.

The arrival of a firstborn son in a Muslim Arab family means his mother can update her identity as *umm*, "mother of," while a new father can take the honorific title *abu*, "father of," using the name of his eldest son. True, many "abus" and "ibns" are actually named after their grandfathers or clans. But there is little point in denying that this custom is in keeping with a Middle East in which, in the words of *The Lion Handbook to the Bible*, "childlessness was always regarded as a calamity, and one's happiness was proportionate (so it was said) to the number of children, particularly sons."

Is the desire for children a basic human instinct? Would I have been distressed by my childlessness in the absence of theological and cultural pressures? After all, religious traditions notwithstanding, nature itself seems to be in favor of procreation. It puts sexual desire into us, which often leads to intercourse, which often leads to pregnancy, regardless of a couple's intentions. Some may view procreation through a Darwinian lens, focusing on the "selfishness" of the genes themselves in their insistence on being passed on. Religion adds a dimension, sanctifying that which comes naturally in nature.

Egypt, Jordan, or (non-Arab) Pakistan. But even in wealthier Kuwait and Saudi Arabia, the science of IVF can sometimes be seen as clashing with the strictures of Sunni Islam. A married couple may undergo treatment so long as no use is made of third-party sperm or eggs. In non-Arab, Shi'ite Iran, third-party donors are permitted, though the children are seen as "adopted" for purposes of Islamic jurisprudence.

The truth is that becoming a parent was not something I had always longed for – and even when it was denied to me, I still found myself somewhat ambivalent. Part of me was afraid of bringing a child into this world and taking on the responsibility of being a father. I had no idea how to be a father. And what if my marriage didn't work out?

Moreover, it had been clear to me for some time that what I needed, far more than being a parent, was to be in a lasting and nurturing relationship. Which is why my marriage to Lisa is actually far more important to me than whether or not I have children. But I don't lead my life in a vacuum. The more confident I felt in my marriage, and the more I came to understand how much Lisa wanted to be a mother, the more important the idea of children became to me. Like the patriarchs before me, I wanted to see her wish granted.

Chapter 5

Go Read Camus

Les Farber is smart-alecky, his sentences replete with what I first take to be a self-deprecating candor, mixed with bravado. Later it dawns on me he must have found the topic of his childlessness difficult to talk about. At 64, Les lives a comfortable life in the Bronx, though his accent has a touch of New England twang. "I'm wasting my life," he declares, almost as soon as we sit down.

Since taking early retirement from a well-paid civil service job, his main activity nowadays is providing eldercare for his spry 90-year-old mother, who lives a few blocks away. The truth is she really doesn't need him all that much. She plays bridge four days a week, and still drives locally. His married brother encourages him to get on with his life, maybe travel more. Les half-heartedly pursues photography as a hobby.

Plainly, Les is in a funk. He's a self-confessed procrastinator. Brainy but not driven, he grew up middle class, mostly on Long Island. At work, he sailed through the ranks and served as acting commissioner of a major city agency. But it was a no-brainer for Les to leave it all behind and take the proffered early retirement package.

Growing up, Les says he and his dad had a good, even close, relationship. "He had polio as a kid, so our bond was not of the physically active kind. He wasn't sappy in the least. He could be funny, and acerbic. He had an edge, but behind it was a nice guy." Les could have been talking about himself.

He claims not to be angry at himself, just disappointed. "When I think about my childlessness, it feels like a failure. I believe in propagation of the tribe. I just haven't managed to do it."

Every childless man has a story, and maybe what strikes me about Les is that his seems so desultory.

"I came very close to having a child. I once dated this French woman who had come to New York on municipal business. I was assigned to show her around, and one thing led to another. She'd come to NY often on vacation and we dated long-distance for about a year and a half. I knew it wasn't going to go anywhere – she was a nice enough person, but she wasn't Jewish."

Then she got pregnant. There were complications. This happened at a time when France was being hit by a general strike, and Les could not get to her. Next thing he heard, she had miscarried in the second trimester. The doctors did not know why. "Upon reflection, it was good news and bad news," he says. "But the anticipation of fatherhood had been something separate from good or bad. I was ambivalent. 'Wow. I am going to be a dad,' I thought. On the other hand, I was going to be a dad with someone I didn't really want to be a dad with.'"

In retrospect, Les realizes that the miscarriage may have been a kind of blessing. "She'd waltz in from Paris and she'd stay with me; it was good, easy, comfortable. But when I got to know her better, when I had to live with her, she became less nice. And really, I didn't want to spend all my life with this person." All the same, after she lost the baby, Les invited his girlfriend to New York to recuperate. Only afterwards did he break it off. She was so hurt she threw a chair at him. "So, the fact that the relationship would have failed anyway ameliorates the loss of my potential fatherhood."

Like several other men I spoke with, Les wants me to know he's just fine in the fertility department; that only his reluctance to make some kind of life plan is at the root of his childlessness. And like those other men, Les professes to like kids. He concurs when I suggest that children can give life meaning. But he sounds more bitter than philosophical when he concludes that life – with or without children – basically has no meaning.

"Go read Albert Camus," he says.

I vaguely recall that Camus was some kind of nihilist. Or was he the French guy who was the existentialist? Or was that Sartre? Les says he identifies with Camus's core belief that happiness is transitory – in fact, that the entire human condition is transient. What seems to bother Camus is the unfairness of death.[1] Later, I stumble upon the fact that Camus's father was killed in World War 1 and that he grew up essentially fatherless.

Is there a connection between existentialism and fatherlessness? The absence of a father provides a degree of freedom but also the added burden of early responsibility. This freedom can be a source of anguish. And a few religious polemicists have tried to associate atheism with fatherlessness.

"I see the purpose of life as being self-perpetuation," Les continues, "but it's nothing more than that. We're spinning around in a little globe in the middle of infinite vastness, and we're all alone. Even if we have kids, within two generations we're forgotten; it means nothing."

Les readily concedes that he'd be more contented if he were a believer, if he could envision himself as part of something bigger.

---

1. "Well, then I'll die. Sooner than other people, obviously. But everybody knows that life isn't worth living. And when it came down to it, I wasn't unaware of the fact that it doesn't matter very much whether you die at thirty or at seventy since, in either case, other men and women will naturally go on living, for thousands of years even. Nothing was plainer, in fact. It was still only me who was dying, whether it was now or in twenty years' time." Albert Camus, *The Stranger* (New York: Vintage Books, 1946). Two other things strike me as pertinent about Camus: He married and fathered two children; and whatever his feelings about life's futility, he dabbled in moderation.

"It is not particularly comforting to believe life is, essentially, meaning-less. I would prefer to have a take on human life that wasn't so stark."

Me too, I think as I listen to him talk. As if reading my mind, Les makes an effort to be more upbeat. He tells me about his two adult nieces and one college-age nephew, with whom "I can't claim to have a close relationship." Then, grasping at straws, he adds, "The nephew, my sister's son, I'm maybe closer with. He's my child by proxy, though I don't want to overstate it. He was born via IVF, so there is no dad in the picture. He's studying art in college. I'm hoping one day he'll come to New York and stay with me. I have a spare room, and he can take in all the museums."

Chapter 6

Be Not Like the Shakers

I f you're feeling forlorn on a Saturday night – and want to keep it that way – here's a movie streaming suggestion: *Children of Men* (2006), based on P.D. James's dystopian novel set in a near-future England where women have mysteriously lost the ability to become pregnant. It reminded me somewhat of Margaret Atwood's *The Handmaid's Tale*, which offers a nightmarish peek into a world of controlled procreation. While James's and Atwood's imagined futures are well-contrived, the plain reality is that childlessness is rising.[1]

Bear with me while I crunch some numbers. About 20 percent of American women will never have any children. As for American men, a CDC survey found that by age 44, 22 percent had not fathered a child.[2]

---

1. "Childlessness Up Among All Women; Down Among Women with Advanced Degrees," *Pew Research*, June 25, 2010.
2. See "Fertility, Contraception, and Fatherhood," http://www.cdc.gov/nchs/data/series/sr_23/sr23_026.pdf.

Over in Britain, a recent survey of women born between 1956 and 1960 found that some 17 percent were childless.[3] Today, the US fertility rate stands at 64.1 births per 1000 for women aged 15–44, which reflects a continuing downward trend.[4] Incidentally, 40 percent of the births are out of wedlock, which raises all sorts of issues about increasing numbers of children who will grow up in homes without dads. The birthrate fell by 6 percent just between 2007 and 2010 for US-born women.[5]

The average American couple makes 1.89 babies. This means there are not enough children to replace their parents. The UK figure is 1.82; Greece 1.48 and Germany 1.41, Japan 1.20, and Korea 1.23. In fact, in most developed countries the statistics indicate birthrates well below replacement levels. In Canada, this trend translates into a staggering 44.5 percent of couples being "without children" compared to 39.2 percent with children. In Australia, one in eight men aged 45 to 59 is childless, whether by choice or circumstance.[6]

Plainly, childlessness, voluntary and involuntary, is a noteworthy, worrisome trend in the West.[7] Why do I say worrisome? *The Economist* has pointed out that in two decades a low US birthrate combined with a decline in immigration could upend the economy's ratio of workers to retirees. By 2050, those 65 and over will comprise

---

3. See "One in five women stays childless because of modern lifestyle," http://www.telegraph.co.uk/news/uknews/5637417/One-in-five-women-stay-childless-because-of-modern-lifestyle.html.

4. In the year I was born, 1954, the birthrate was 118.1 per 1,000.

5. "Motherhood When Times Are Tough," *The New York Times*, December 6, 2012.

6. For Canada, see "Trend of couples not having children just plain selfish," *National Post*, September 19, 2012. Regarding Australia, see "What happens when you can't have kids?" *The Sunday Morning Herald*, April 26, 2014.

7. In contrast, many of the poorest countries with the highest birthrates are Muslim, with Niger and Mali in the lead. Today's global Muslim population is forecast to increase by about 35 percent in the next twenty years, even if at a slower pace than in previous decades. In the wake of the Islamist takeover in Egypt, for instance, the birthrate soared to its highest point in decades. Whatever the demographic impact of the July 2013 military coup led by General Abdel Fattah al-Sisi, which ousted Mohammed Morsi's Muslim Brotherhood regime, the country's population had reached 85 million by the summer of 2013. In London, with its burgeoning Muslim population, the most popular name for newborn boys is Muhammad.

22 percent of the population. "A falling birth rate and much slower immigration presage long-term trouble ahead."[8]

Among the Jewish people, we've long reached the point where Jews are legitimately worried about their dwindling numbers. On the one hand, we face a seemingly irreparable tribal rift among the world's 15 million Jews over how to define Jewishness. At the same time, huge swaths of young Jews worldwide are marrying out and not raising their offspring in a Jewish framework.[9] And on top of it all, we are transitioning from being an ancient people to also being a graying one, with 36 as the median age of Jews worldwide, compared to a global figure of 28.[10]

In my former hometown of New York, the non-Orthodox "tend to marry late, bear few children, and intermarry at high rates," according to historian Jack Wertheimer in his essay, "First New York's Jews, Then America's?"[11] His analysis of the fertility data shows that the Orthodox minority (currently one-fifth of the tri-state area's Jewish households, but soon to become demographically dominant in the city proper) "are raising more than 60 percent of Jewish children under the age of 18." In an earlier October 2005 *Commentary* essay, "Jews and the Jewish Birthrate," Wertheimer called attention to the fact that Jewish American women are less procreative than their non-Jewish counterparts. Meanwhile, the *2000 National Jewish Population Survey* found that more than half of 30- to 34-year-old Jewish women are childless; that's roughly double the percentage in the general American population.[12] At age 44, 26 percent of American Jewish women are childless.[13]

---

8. "America's demographic squeeze," *The Economist*, December 15, 2012.
9. In some of the largest Diaspora communities, the rate of Jews marrying non-Jews hovers around 50 percent. See, for example, "Intermarriage rates among Diaspora Jews at all-time high," *Yediot Aharonot*, November 17, 2010.
10. *Pew Research*, December 18, 2012.
11. *Commentary*, September 1, 2012.
12. "Low Fertility Key to 2000 Census," *New York Jewish Week*, October 11, 2002. My own take is that if the driving force of this Orthodox demographic surge turns out to be the predominantly insular non-Zionist and economically disadvantaged *ḥaredi* sector – while the numbers themselves are intrinsically welcome – they will have little interest in sustaining Jewish civilization as we know it.
13. See *NJPS: Marriage and Fertility*, United Jewish Communities.

In The Netherlands, about 33 percent of Jewish women born since 1955 are childless at age 40, and the percentage is rising. In England, 36 percent of Jews live alone, and 32 percent of couples live in homes with no children.[14]

There is conflicting evidence about whether childless adults are lonelier than those who are parents, though the disconcerting suggestion has been raised that we face premature death.[15] Predictably, as we childless people grow older, research shows we are more likely than parents to live alone or in an institution.[16] Couples who have tried and failed to become pregnant through IVF may actually be doomed to shorter life-spans than those who succeeded.[17] And it appears that childless men, at least in Australia, earn less than those who are fathers.[18]

A childless couple in Beijing (their only son had died) has been unable to find a nursing home willing to accept them.[19] And in the US, lawyers are encouraging millions of childless American baby boomers to appoint healthcare proxies to handle medical decisions, should they become incapacitated.[20]

A few summers back, Lisa and I visited the Shaker Village in Hancock, Massachusetts. Most people who've heard of the Shakers know that

---

14. For The Netherlands, see "Around the Jewish World New Survey of Dutch Jewry Shows Few Marriages or Kids, Much Divorce," *JTA*, November 1, 2001. For England, see "Jews in Britain: A Snapshot from the 2001 Census," *Berman Jewish Policy Archive*, May 18, 2007.

15. See "Loneliness and Depression in Middle and Old Age: Are the Childless More Vulnerable?" *The Journal of Gerontology*, June 3, 1998. "Childless couples have higher risk of dying prematurely but adopting may reduce chances of an early death," *Daily Mail*, December 6, 2012.

16. "Characteristics of Older Childless Persons and Parents' Cross-National Comparisons," *Journal of Family Issues*, October 2007.

17. "Childlessness Tied to Higher Death Rate," *MedPage Today*, December 11, 2012.

18. "Fathers earn almost a fifth more salary than childless men," News.com.au, December 24, 2012.

19. "Nursing homes reject childless couple," *China Daily*, January 31, 2013.

20. "Childless Baby Boomers: Who Will Care for the Caregiver?" Fawcett & Fawcett Attorneys at Law, http://fawcettlaw.com/.

they crafted classically simple, clean-lined wooden furniture. Today, the village functions as a kind of living museum, and we took the afternoon to walk around, learning about their craft in addition to how they raised livestock and planted crops.

In 1774, a woman known as "Mother Ann Lee" settled the Shakers, formerly known as the United Society of Believers in Christ's Second Coming, in the New World and founded multiple utopian religious communes with strict conventions about how Christians ought to live their lives – one key tenet being celibacy. There were maybe 5,000 Shakers in America during the mid-1800s, concentrated mostly in the Northeast; today they've almost entirely died out.[21]

Plainly, the Shakers did not have a blueprint for continuity. Walking that summer day through their village, I found myself thinking of the Second Temple-era Essenes, a quasi-monastic Dead Sea sect of spiritual, apocalyptic, and messianic Jews who, like the Shakers, also embraced the idea of celibacy. Had Jews followed in their footsteps en masse, we'd be where the Shakers are today, minus the legacy of nice furniture.

But clearly, Israelis are not taking their cue from the Essenes. Israel ranks first among the thirty-four-member Organization of Economic Cooperation and Development states, a roster of the world's most advanced countries, with 2.75 births per woman.

Child-friendly, child-encouraging Israel, where I have made my home for nearly two decades, produces 3.03 children per family: broken down, that's 2.07 for majority non-Orthodox households; 6.53 among the ultra-Orthodox; 3.51 among Muslims; 2.19 for Christian Arabs; and 2.33 among the Druze.

Looking at Israeli families with children, only one percent have just a single child; 12 percent have two children; 40 percent have three; 25 percent have four; and 14 percent have five or more.

As you might expect, religiosity and fertility are correlated: an average of eight children delivers high status among the

---

21. See "Hancock Shaker Village: A Brief History," http://hancockshakervillage.org/shakers/history/.

ultra-Orthodox – who comprise about 10 percent of the population, though they tend to be less well-off economically. Among immigrant groups interested in acculturating to the Israeli mainstream, we're seeing that fertility is increasing for those from the former Soviet Union, where it had been artificially low, while decreasing among Ethiopians, where it had been traditionally high.[22] For those concerned about Jewish numbers, all this procreation is encouraging. At the same time, for men and women without children, it can be isolating.

I have no problem with survey results showing that an overwhelming majority of Israelis think the greatest joy in life is watching children grow up. I'm less thrilled that my compatriots also believe that childless people have empty lives.[23] That this attitude is understandable doesn't make it any less condescending. And it may help explain why some women feel an unremitting pressure to persevere with IVF at great personal cost even after more than a dozen failures.[24]

Maybe it's all part of a Middle East cultural mindset.

When I worked at *The Jerusalem Post*, I was on cordial terms with an Arab custodian named Daoud, with whom I'd exchange daily pleasantries and gripes. Daoud had seen Lisa visiting me at the office, so he knew I was married and, not unreasonably, assumed I had children. "How's the family? Children all well?" he'd ask. My response was a generic "*Alhamdulillah*," Thank God. For some reason, and this is hardly Daoud's fault, I could never work up enough courage to say, "Look, Daoud, actually we have no kids." Playing along seemed the path of least resistance. After a while, Daoud began asking if I had any grandchildren yet. "*Alhamdulillah*," I said.

Around the same time, I had started seeing a new dentist. On my second visit, he politely, nonchalantly, asked after my kids, which put me in a quandary. I'd already told him on my initial visit that

22. Under Soviet rule, the Russian birthrate was at or slightly below replacement level. When the regime collapsed in 1991 and daily life was torn asunder, the birthrate fell to the extent that deaths exceeded births. Now births are picking up again.

23. Y. Lavee and R. Katz, "The Family in Israel: Between Tradition and Modernity," *Marriage & Family Review*, 34 (2003) (1–2): 193–217.

24. "Israel is the World Leader in Fertility," *Haaretz* (Hebrew), April 15, 2013.

I had no children. So I bit the air-suction tube and said one more time: "It's just me and my wife. No kids." What a relief it was to say those words. We've now been together for a dozen years, and Dr. Sammy only asks after Lisa or makes pleasant small talk about work, the weather, and mutual acquaintances. There were never any further queries about my non-existent children.

But my split-second dilemma that day points to a larger question: How much emotional energy should you invest in setting people straight when they ask after the children you don't have? Especially when they ask a second and third time in the "Hihowareyou? Howrthekids?" fashion.

To be childless is – forgive the expression – pregnant with consequences. And coming to grips with it is a life-long process. It's something I feel, for instance, when I attend a *brit mila* (circumcision) ceremony, a bar or bat mitzva; I feel it in synagogue when the children are dressed in Purim holiday costumes, and in the living room of a friend's house as we gather to toast the induction of his son into the Israeli army. Sometimes I even feel it at weddings, when the rabbi blesses the bride and groom standing under the canopy with "May you merit building a home of faith in Israel." "Home," means children, of course.

Yet the simple fact is that many men don't have children. It could be the result of chance, choice, or infertility. Not much research has been done on what it means to a man's identity not to be a father. But there are two studies published decades apart that explore the feelings of infertile men.

The earlier is by a Canadian graduate student named Russell Webb, who interviewed a group of young men recently told they were biologically incapable of fathering children.[25] For many it seemed like

---

25. As far as I know, there is not a whole lot of work being carried out in the social sciences on childless men. Webb's 1994 Master's thesis, "The Experience and Meaning of Infertility for Biologically Childless Infertile Men," was path-breaking. In 2014, Dr. Liberty Barnes at the University of Cambridge made a major new contribution to the field with *Conceiving Masculinity: Male Infertility, Medicine, and Identity* published by Temple University Press (see below). Doctoral student

the end of the line. Webb found that the cohort he studied initially experienced a sense of grief and loss, followed by feelings of powerlessness, inadequacy, betrayal, isolation, foreboding, and, finally and mercifully, the conviction that each individually would somehow overcome and survive.

Webb's findings rang true for me. I spent years subliminally grieving for the son or daughter I would never have. I, too, felt a sense of powerlessness and inadequacy because what came naturally, effortlessly, to just about everyone else was beyond my reach. Didn't that somehow make me less of a man?

Bob, one of the subjects whom Webb interviewed, felt it did: "I felt unmanly, inadequate, and powerless when I compared myself to other men who had children." Lester, another subject, felt betrayed that none of his church friends ever raised the issue with him. "Nobody knew what to do with us. And so it was just ignored. Not everybody knew, but the ones that did know – nobody talked about it. And nobody worked anything through with us."

Sean, a third interviewee, spoke of his loneliness: "We thought nobody had this issue; that we were the only couple in the whole world that has had to deal with such a terrible, dramatic thing as infertility."

Like the men Webb met, I felt betrayed as I wondered if maybe, contrary to the repeated assurances I'd received, I had been exposed to dangerous levels of radiation while working my way through graduate school at the New York City Health Department in the 1980s. Might this low-level exposure have contributed to my inability to produce healthy sperm?

I also felt a sense of isolation. Aside from Lisa, there was no friend to talk to – no one who could understand on an experiential level what I was going through.

Ann Dalzell has been working at the University of Bristol compiling testimonies of childless men with the aim of understanding "how the individual makes sense of, and creates meaning within, the stories he tells." And another doctoral student, Robin Hadley of Keele University, has done research to show that "childless men can be just as broody as women – and, indeed, are more prone to feeling depressed and angry about not having kids."

Then there was the latent dread at social functions, with work colleagues, congregants at my synagogue, and anyone else I was meeting for the first time, over how to handle the kids question. And the more generalized anxieties: Did Lisa's parents hold me responsible? Who would take an interest in us when we are older and less able to fend for ourselves?

Yet, sure enough, like Webb's interview subjects, I gradually began to make peace with what had initially felt like an unjust sentence. And there is no question in my mind that the counseling sessions Lisa and I had with Edna were vital to that process. But more than that, I survived because I didn't feel Lisa thought any less of me. We both felt that nothing was more important than keeping our relationship intact and strengthening what we had together – children or no children.

The latest and most comprehensive work on childless men is by medical sociologist Liberty Barnes. In *Conceiving Masculinity: Male Infertility, Medicine, and Identity*,[26] she explores how being childless affects a man's character. It's true that, "when a heterosexual couple experience childlessness, it is the woman's body that is visibly and conspicuously not pregnant, stigmatizing *her* as infertile," while "infertile men enjoy a good amount of invisibility."

But men are not impervious to the keen sense of sadness that comes with infertility. "Infertility is not life-threatening," writes Barnes, "but it is life-defining." She demonstrates how "strength, courage, power" are tied to virility in the popular imagination. "A real man can get the sex he wants and impregnate a woman when he so desires," writes Barnes. Men who "have balls" are courageous; while the expression "shooting blanks" connotes helplessness. Asked to characterize his own infertility, one interview subject told Barnes, "If I was on an island with one million girls, we would all be dead within the next 100 years, and there would be no one left on the island."

Not being able to have children when you want to is "sad" and "scary" because it's "like you're not in charge of your own life,"

---

26. Philadelphia: Temple University Press, 2014.

another interviewee told Barnes. That's why men are willing to try just about any medical advance to fix the problem.

For men with partners, sex can become a symbolic reminder of the inability to make babies. But after the initial shock wears off men tend to gain perspective. "Just because my plumbing got messed up," said one, "doesn't make me any less of a man." Men find different ways to cope. Several childless men I know have become obsessive custodians of their family trees, as though trying to compensate for their own missing branches.

Marcus Pfeffer, a married, fifty-something property investor living in New York, is one such man. He introduces himself, bluntly, as having "no biological future." It is clear, though, that he takes immense pleasure in being the family historian. Yet with strangers his family-tree interests provide no buffer. "When I go to a new shul," Marcus relates, "what's the second question people ask? 'Are you married?' is the first. 'Yes, we're married.' Then, it's 'Do you have children?' When I reply, 'No,' there are those who politely change the subject. Other times, I get a stony silence. The worst is when you get sympathy that borders on the maudlin. I suspect most people when they find out are privately sanctimonious."

Like every man I encountered in writing this book, Marcus had never decided to be childless. It just happened. Born in 1959, the younger of two brothers, Marcus was raised in an affluent home on the Upper West Side of Manhattan. After graduating from the London School of Economics, he returned to New York, where he went directly into the family's substantial real estate business.

He was 28 when he married Bernadette, who came from a French-speaking, Swiss-Jewish family. Despite his traditional upbringing, he lets me know, he had his share of girlfriends in his prior existence. He gives me to understand, without wanting to say too much, that his own fertility is not in question. "I don't have a child out there in the world, but there could have been one."

Shortly after they became engaged in 1987, Bernadette was diagnosed with colon cancer. But although she soon made a complete recovery, doctors told her it would be unwise for her to become pregnant for five years. That did not seem like it would pose a problem – he was 28 at the time, she was 26. Then, quite suddenly – less than two years into the marriage – Bernadette's mother died of cancer of the uterus, an illness doctors had assured her she'd beaten years earlier. To add to the family's woes, Bernadette's sister soon also died of cancer. Bernadette became less confident that her own cancer would not return. So she and her husband decided to wait just a little bit longer – still not deliberately planning against having children.

"But at some point, due to fortunate circumstances, we found ourselves financially comfortable and went into a certain pattern of life. We were almost – I won't say happy – content with our existence without children. I suppose, as time went on, we made a decision, without stating it as baldly as that, that we wouldn't have children. It was not Plan A."

Physically, the couple was capable of making a baby, which has left Marcus, more than Bernadette, ambivalent about their decision not to. He was worried that he'd drive himself – and any child – mad because he's such a perfectionist. "If I were to have a child, I would be scared he would not live up to my expectations. In a sense, I was kind of glad that circumstances had influenced our decision about having children."

Ultimately, he tells me, he came to see not having children as a facet in his proudly nonconformist life. His affluence and business interests have allowed Marcus to straddle two worlds comfortably – one modern Orthodox, the other non-Jewish. He knows that fellow Orthodox Jews might see his childlessness as a misfortune. "I meet someone and when I say I have no children, they look at me as a hapless unfortunate. Sometimes, I feel that too. But I am childless out of selfishness, if that's the right word. I can't embrace the view within Judaism that childlessness is a punishment because I have, in a sense, elected for it, albeit with some misgivings."

Marcus thinks of himself as a believing Jew – not just as some-one who is faithful to ritual. "I believe in a God who micro manages our lives and I think God has allowed me to live this way without being too critical of me. There is free will, but at the same time we're governed by a sort of spiritual force.

"I am very conscious that I am not a saint and I don't do anything extraordinary, but I do try to do my bit for *tikkun olam* – the Jewish impulse to make the world a better place. To compensate for the fact that I am not doing it through children, I give not a small amount of charity and put myself out for different things."

Like many other men who have no children of their own, Marcus takes extra interest in his nieces and nephews. "My brother has five children, and my wife's sister has four, so that compensates, legacy-wise, for the fact that we don't have kids. Had my brother not had children, I would have probably had to think harder about having children, maybe pushed more to have a child of my own. I am very close to his children and I have a paternal instinct, there is no question."

Adoption has never been in the cards. "I never wanted it; never wanted anybody else's – maybe because we could have children. I've always thought if we are going to have a child, we should produce our own."

As we wrap up our talk, he admits to being "somewhat confused" about his childlessness. "I also feel somewhat embarrassed, in retrospect, in my religious milieu; when I say we don't have children in my other world, I don't think twice about it.

"I said Kaddish for my parents twice a day without ever missing for two years. I am mindful that when I leave this world, there is no one to say Kaddish for me."

Chapter 7

Amen Party

From Bible stories to hasidic folktales, Judaism's message about infertility is that it is not some unfortunate medical condition, nor just plain bad luck, but a spiritual defect, retribution for sin. The Book of Exodus states that no Jewish woman *in God's favor* will ever be barren or even miscarry (Ex. 23:26). Scripture is explicit: "Thou shalt be blessed above all peoples; there shall not be male nor female barren among you, or among your cattle" (Deut. 7:14). But only "if you do obey these rules and observe them carefully" (Deut. 7:12).

These are not proclamations that can be easily read as metaphors. *Vocatus atque non vocatus deus aderit* – bidden or not bidden, God will be present.[1] And nowhere, paradoxically, is God more omnipresent than in the childless home.

---

1. The Latin, incidentally, is the inscription psychologist Carl Jung (1875–1961) had etched in stone over his doorway in Switzerland.

God owns my childlessness. It is one area where He can't easily be let off the hook. *He's* the one, after all, who made such a big deal about childlessness. For if, as my historic 1902 copy of the *Jewish Encyclopedia* practically taunts, "To be without children is regarded as the greatest curse" in Judaism, then how am I supposed to de-link my relationship with God from my childlessness?

For better or worse, God is central to the equation. His fingerprints are all over infertility. God has a history of wielding childlessness as a bludgeon to intimidate or punish Israel. Reflect on how we entreat God on Yom Kippur: "And for the sins for which we are liable to be cut off and childless."

Childlessness and punishment go hand-in-hand. Thinking about having sex with your aunt or sister-in-law? The consequences will be childlessness (Lev. 20:20–21).

The Pater incessantly urges me to plead for a child at the gravesite of a *tzaddik*. In his world, praying at the tomb of a righteous individual is considered efficacious. While Rachel's Tomb has no real competition for those bent on what I call *graving*, the Tomb of Shimon Bar Yochai, the first-century sage reputed to have authored the mystical book of the Zohar, is probably a close second. Of course, journeying to the Ukraine gravesite of Rebbe Naḥman, founder of the Breslov hasidic dynasty, wouldn't hurt either.

Some women travel to Jerusalem's Har Hamenuḥot cemetery to pray at the grave of Miriam Mizraḥi, popularly known as Miriam the Laundress, a childless ultra-Orthodox woman who once worked for a revered Jerusalem rabbi. She pleaded for the rabbi to bless her so she could have a child. He demurred, she persisted. Finally, he cautioned her that Heaven had decreed she remain childless. Miriam argued that everything was in the hands of God, and she would take her chances. So the sage reluctantly gave her the blessing. Tragically, the child died before his bar mitzva. In the wake of his death, and until her own death in 1963, Miriam was said to have devoted herself to random acts of kindness. She has achieved a certain posthumous celebrity by purportedly appearing in the dreams of former neighbors, urging them to usher childless women to her grave to pray and give charity in her memory. The results for those who do so are said to be good.[2]

Even before anyone *schleps* from cemetery to cemetery, however, couples who can't conceive are encouraged to rule out obvious supernatural deficiencies – an imperfect mezuza, a flawed *ketuba* marriage contract, a lackadaisical approach to the laws of "family purity," meaning abstinence from sexual relations during and immediately following the woman's menstrual cycle. Apparently, a pious frame of mind, in conjunction with reciting esoteric prayers, can also facilitate bringing children into the world.

The Lubavitcher Rebbe, who himself had no children, famously was able to pinpoint ethical lapses that, once removed, opened the way to a successful pregnancy. His multitude of followers believe he still has that capability and presently make their supplications at his Queens, NY, tomb.[3] What went through his mind as a pastor to the infertile? God only knows. In a textbook example of cognitive dissonance, his followers are said to believe that the Rebbe's childlessness is further proof that he is the Messiah.

Jewish folklorists have tried to get God off the hook by ascribing infertility troubles not to a hard-hearted, chastising, micromanaging Deity, but to autonomous malevolent supernatural forces.[4] In such cases, overcoming the demons might require anything from eating mandrakes, apples, roosters, or fish, to touching a woman already with child, swallowing the foreskin of a newly circumcised

---

2. Recalling the story of Rachel, perhaps there is an element in Judaism that links persistent demands for children, that are granted by God, with a subsequent death. As if to say, be careful what you wish for…

3. Chabad maintains that the Rebbe remains the Messiah, which is why his death in 1994 at Beth Israel Hospital is theologically referred to as the "transmission." I do not know any ranking Chabad personality who speaks of the Rebbe explicitly in the past tense. The fascinatingly schismatic nature of Chabad is best described by Prof. David Berger in *The Rebbe, the Messiah, and the Scandal of Orthodox Indifference*, (London: Littman Library of Jewish Civilization, 2001). Also of interest is Samuel Heilman and Menachem Friedman, *The Rebbe: The Life and Afterlife of Menachem Mendel Schneerson*, (Princeton, NJ: Princeton University Press, 2011).

4. See, for example, *Encyclopedia Judaica*, vol. 6, p. 1401.

infant, biting the *pitom* (tip) of an *etrog* (citron), or drinking water with which a corpse has been ritually washed.

Still not pregnant or impregnating?

Try crawling under a gestating mare, gazing at a ritual circumcision knife, drinking the water used by the *kohanim* (priests) before the priestly blessings on Yom Kippur, or fondling, then eating, the willow leaf used during the *Shemini Atzeret* festival.[5]

You're asking, can this possibly reflect Judaism's *contemporary* attitude toward childlessness? All I know is that in the face of this accumulated, let us call it "canon," there is only silence.

This isn't to say there aren't ostensibly normal folks willing to give testimony that the hocus-pocus works.

Having gormlessly failed to navigate my way through a warren of Tel Aviv-Jaffa pathways and steps, I espy Erez Gottfried standing casually barefooted outside his cottage apartment, phone in hand, directing me to the last stages of our rendezvous. I am now 25 minutes late, but he doesn't seem bothered. Nor does he seem weighed down by his childlessness. Far from it.

Erez, 33, and his wife Donna, 32, both grew up in affluent New York City suburbs. They met through serendipity when he called her for information about a mutual friend. They fell in love and shared an unabashed passion for making money. Cashing in on their business, the couple moved to Israel five years ago with the aim of bolstering their already strong Orthodox Jewish way of life.

We meet in Erez's living room with its stunning view of the Mediterranean Sea. The first order of business is an introduction. Donna is not at home, but Wally, the couple's cuddly white bunny rabbit, is – and carries on munching on his vegetables. Only afterwards does it dawn on me that Wally is a symbol of fertility – as in "to breed like rabbits."

Erez tells me he's spent more than seven years on personal growth and what he calls "entrepreneurial thinking." He works in business development and marketing, travels around the world

---

5. Ibid.

"helping people take their lives to the next level," and manages a variety of volunteer projects from couples' counseling to organizing bone-marrow drives. Erez exudes confidence, so I have no inhibitions about getting right down to business. What does he think of Judaism's unforgiving attitude toward the childless as *akar* – Hebrew for "uprooted," a kind of dead man walking – unfit to lead prayers on the High Holy Days, and with no place in the World to Come?

"I don't view Judaism's attitude as unforgiving or mean-spirited," he replies with the calm, nonjudgmental assurance of a self-help aficionado. "Take the term *akar*.[6] A farmer who runs out of seed that he needs to plant his garden – well, to call him an 'uprooted' farmer is not bashing the man personally. *Tachlis*, practically speaking, the farmer simply doesn't have seed to plant for next year's crop. So I don't see *akar* as a word that is personal, or decimating, or horrible – I see it from the perspective of creating lineage, creating history. The Jewish people see ourselves as the Children of Abraham, having received the Torah collectively with Moses at Sinai. The idea of not being able to continue that line really does amount to an uprooting of our continuity."

Erez speaks with an assured light touch, though his message is hardnosed.

"As for being dead,[7] the Talmud means, I think, that people who have no children are in a place where they don't get a certain fulfillment – just like the blind are 'dead' because they can't experience a whole dimension of life. True, a childless man can't be a *ḥazan* leading the services on Rosh HaShana or Yom Kippur, but what's key here is that the High Holy Days are a time of year when we look to God as our Father, so it's a whole relationship we're creating.

"God punishes Israel with barrenness on a national level – He doesn't punish the individual person."

---

6. I'll have more to say about *akar* in Chapter 11, "Kaddish'l."
7. "Rabbi Joshua ben Levi said: A man who is childless is accounted as dead" (Nedarim 64b). For further elaboration, see Chapter 11.

I marvel at his equanimity, and ask, "Given your outlook, and at 33, do you, in fact, consider yourself a childless man?"

"No," he replies. "Anything can always happen. This is life. Let me tell you some things, and ultimately, I will have a punch line."

And so I settle in to hear his story.

"Donna and I have been married 11 years. The first two years we practiced birth control because we were concentrating on making money. It was obvious there would be kids – later. For the past eight years or so, we've been actively trying to get pregnant. When we realized it wasn't going to be simple we began exploring and discovered that Donna had polycystic ovary syndrome, which makes having babies a bit more challenging. All along, Donna and I have been open about not having kids, and we talk about this stuff. We don't have to look good."

Months before they moved to Israel, Erez belatedly discovered that Donna's ovaries weren't the only fertility obstacle to overcome. He himself had a low sperm count due to varicose veins in one of his testicles. To fix the problem, Erez underwent a painless procedure, followed by a torturously agonizing recovery period. To further raise his sperm count, he also tried acupuncture, Chinese herbs, intensified his regimen of self-development, and began living more healthily. Sure enough, Erez's sperm count shifted into the normal range.

After arriving in Tel Aviv, they tried intrauterine insemination (IUI), the most straightforward of fertility interventions. Doctors inserted Erez's sperm directly into Donna's uterus, using a catheter. The idea was to increase the number of sperm that reached Donna's fallopian tubes and thereby boost the chances of fertilization. After three or four failed tries, they decided on a different approach. "We were really proactive. There was no 'Why me?', just 'What can we do?'

"Along the journey, we went up to Jerusalem to the Western Wall for forty days to pray. The number forty is a *segula*, a spiritual technique. We recited our prayer request repeatedly, every day, for forty consecutive days. We also sought, and received, blessings from friends and from rabbis. What's more, we did juice cleanses, a detox diet, colon cleanses, more Chinese herbs, more acupuncture."

At one point, he recalls, they went to an Orthodox agency that counsels couples with fertility problems, only to discover that they were better informed than their counselor. "There's probably more dead rabbis' graves that we could have gone to and more *segulas* we could have done, but we'd pretty much done everything."

He swiftly dismisses my suggestion that he was looking for an intermediary to facilitate a fertility miracle. "As people of faith, we realized that somehow, in who we were as a couple, there was something stuck. That something spiritual was lacking. We knew that God loves people's prayers. God loves repentance. So, not from a place that God is angry or punishing us, but from a place that, well, maybe we are just missing something in our lives that we could put out there, the result, or the solution, of our effort will be a baby."

Erez also lets me know that he doesn't like the term "childless." "That's a phrase of hopelessness; it turns me into something negative. The guy puffing away is not 'a smoker.' He is someone who smokes cigarettes. His dependency on tobacco does not define his essence.

"Anyway, 2,000 years ago, the idea of not having children was very different from not having children today. I mean, today there are so many options. We had people offering to be surrogate mothers for us, there's IVF, adoption, so many options," he repeats.

He and Donna truly left no supernatural stone unturned. They started baking *challa*, considered still another *segula*, accompanied by relevant prayers. Erez increased his time volunteering. The couple went so far as to "adopt" Donna's dysfunctional 15-year-old kid brother from America for two long years. "We said, 'We don't have kids, let this be proof to you, God, that we're capable of being parents.'

"The reality is that sometimes the 'happy ending' isn't the biblical happy ending of having a child. Sometimes it is just the happy ending of having a great life. As someone who trains people in entrepreneurial thinking and in multidimensional thinking, my assumption is that each of us has hundreds of dimensions to our lives. The dimension of children is just one narrow perspective."

Erez recalls a quote he heard somewhere, "There is no way to happiness. Happiness *is* the way." I look it up later. It is attributed to the Buddha. "And in Judaism we say, '*Ivdu et Hashem beSimḥa*,' that we should serve God in joy. I mean, if you are going to serve God, you might as well do it with happiness."

As to all those irritating Bible references that portray the childless in negative terms, Erez advises – reaching for another idea popular in self-help circles – "Seek not what the people of old did, but rather the intentions behind it." In other words, he explains, let's apply the message of procreation to what we can do. We need to focus on the things that are working, and on staying positive.

Getting back to their own story, he says, "Anyway, Donna had this notion in her head that 'When it is the right time, it's going to come, and I don't want to force it. I'm not looking to inject myself full of hormones.'" But Donna had also told Erez that once she hit 32 years of age, she would do IVF. "That was her cut-off point," Erez tells me. "So here we are at 32 years old – we've finally started to look into IVF." Donna reluctantly made an appointment at their health clinic for a preliminary evaluation.[8] Erez went along with Donna's decision, though at a deeper level he still felt that "my life is as great as it needs to be right now, and I'm going to celebrate what I do have. I'm constantly processing myself – letting go of any bullshit."

To illustrate just how serene he's been, Erez tells me that at the close of Shabbat, to herald in the new week, he and Dona host a communal *Havdala* ceremony. They light a braided candle, pour the sacramental wine, pass around sweet-smelling spices and, in addition, Erez plays the guitar, with Donna accompanying him on the bongo drums. "All of our couple friends come with their kids. There are more kids here than adults!" Erez says pointedly.

It's been a while since I encountered someone so on-message. I had to ask: From whence comes this wellspring of acceptance, quietude, and positivity? I'd like some of it myself.

"I once was a total ass," Erez informs me. But at some point in their entrepreneurial lives, Erez and Donna were introduced to

---

8. Under Israel's system of national health insurance, all citizens must belong to one of several health plans.

something called the Landmark Forum. At the suggestion of a senior colleague, they enrolled in its seminars with the goal of gaining a set of skills that would help them earn even more money. Landmark, though, turned out to be about more than salesmanship. It offered the couple an affirmative message advocating a lifestyle rooted in optimism. The idea spoke to them deeply. One tenet is, "Human behavior is governed by a need to look good." You can be a better person by learning to shed this crippling need.[9]

Tapping into Judaism's optimistic message of salvation and Landmark's idea of self-affirmation, Erez has managed to mesh these two worldviews to the point where he volunteers at a storefront yeshiva in Jaffa and coaches the newly religious in self-improvement.

Still, I find myself tempted to probe just a bit deeper.

When Donna is in synagogue on Rosh HaShana listening to the *haftara* reading, the one set in Shiloh about the barren Hannah and her husband Elkanah, doesn't Erez worry – even a tad – about the narrative's effect on Donna's psyche? To my surprise, he replies, "Actually, this was the first High Holiday period that Donna didn't want to go to shul – she didn't want to see everyone with their little kids. She didn't want to see me up there opening the Torah ark as a *segula*.

"We've been a *kvater*, the couple who carry the 8-day-old infant from his mother to the *mohel* for ritual circumcision, for, like, 14 families," says Erez. Giving the *kvater* honor to a childless couple is intended to confer a blessing that they have children of their own. "We said, 'Let's start nesting a little bit,'" he recalls.

I'm getting mixed signals, but this is starting to sound more in line with my own experience, and with what I've heard from other childless couples. A sense that sometimes you need a time-out from the world of children and child-centric events.

"So we went to the doctor to start the IVF preliminaries. And Donna did a bunch of blood tests."

---

9. Some say Landmark is a cult because it's an offshoot of EST, the self-help craze popular during the 1970s and 1980s; and, in fact, Landmark is run by EST founder Werner Hans Erhard's brother, Harry Rosenberg.

Simultaneously, Donna heard that aspirin had helped a yoga instructor friend of hers conceive, so she started taking aspirin. Another friend traveled to Uman, Ukraine, to pray at Rebbe Nachman's tomb, both for herself and for Donna. "The friend came back pregnant," Erez reports, "which is pretty amazing."

"Anyway, we come back from all the pre-IVF blood tests, and that night was the anniversary of Matriarch Rachel's death, signifying that her soul had reached the highest level of heaven. So Donna, who is a holy woman, goes to Rachel's Tomb in Bethlehem with her now-pregnant friend. They recite thirty-nine specially selected biblical verses of praise to God – packed with mystical meaning. And they organize thirty-nine women, all reciting the prayers of praise, all meditating with our names in mind. Before that, Donna had also organized an 'amen' party in our house, getting twenty women to respond 'amen' to her prayers a hundred times.

"The night after the blood test, Donna comes back from Rachel's Tomb having had a really moving spiritual experience, and she goes on-line to check her blood results. And it provides an HGC reading, but this time there is a number there. There's never been a number before. I'm not really sure what that means," Erez lets his voice trail off.

"We found out two days later that we're pregnant. HGC is a hormone produced in the body during pregnancy. This for the first time in 11 years. At this moment Donna is five months pregnant," Erez reaches his punchline, trying to gauge my reaction.

"Five months pregnant..." I repeat, perplexed. The premise of our interview was how Erez was coping as a childless man. Had there been a miscommunication? Probably not, and I can't help but feel manipulated. My sense is Erez feels it is his mission to share this good news as a testament of what faith can achieve.

Erez goes on. "...and we didn't need to do IVF. It was sort of like the Sacrifice of Isaac. Like God saying, 'I just want to see that you are willing to offer it. And once I know that, you don't have to do it.' At this point, we are just so inspired. It's been a l-o-n-g journey. On top of it all, the baby was actually conceived on Donna's Hebrew birthday," he adds.

"I don't know if any of this fits into what you want to do in your book," Erez allows.

"*Beshaa tova umutzlaḥat*," I say in Hebrew, literally "in a good and auspicious time," offering my own blessing that everything should go well.

Chapter 8

The American Dream

It was not love at first sight.

My parents were set up in 1951 by a fellow named Heizler, a *gabbai* (sexton) on the Lower East Side who probably moonlighted as a *shadkhan* (matchmaker). The introduction almost certainly had an assist from our family's Rabbi Halpern. My father recalls Heizler assuring him that my mother "had money." Perhaps the *gabbai* pointed out that she'd been working as a seamstress for years while living with her mother. A more sophisticated fellow would have quickly figured out that he'd been told a white lie. Not my father. He believed it with *emuna shelema*, complete faith.

In any event, my mother *looked* like she had money. She was pretty, petite, a stylish dresser. She would have talked about summertime visits to a family compound at Kiamesha Lake, New York, where her relative, affectionately known as "Papa Klein," had a farm, complete with horses. One black-and-white photograph of her shows her sitting in an oversized Adirondack wooden chair, on a lawn, wearing a smart pants suit and looking like a young Katharine Hepburn. Some of her mother's family had also scraped together money for a property in Brooklyn. Maybe she wanted to project a moneyed image.

Yvette (Yetta) had come to New York City in 1923, at age nine, from Warsaw accompanied by her mother, Leah, aboard the *ss Mount Clinton* sailing out of Hamburg. Calvin Coolidge was president. Family lore has it that three little girls, Sadie, Betty, and Yetta, were overheard talking on their Warsaw stoop about which of their fathers, already in America, would be first to bring the rest of the family over.

Yetta's father, my grandfather, left for America just before the outbreak of the First World War, in 1914. He had not been a presence during her formative years. That probably was not atypical during the early 1900s, when war, government naturalization rules, and lack of money separated families for extended periods.

In America, Yetta, as she was then still known, did well in school, perfecting an accent-less English and winning awards for her elegant penmanship. She graduated from Public School 63 on East 3rd Street in 1929. In her school album she wrote that her ambition was to be a secretary. She was positively thrilled to enter Washington Irving High School, located around the corner from the famous S. Klein's Department Store in downtown Manhattan's Union Square. Yet her home life didn't reflect the standard trajectory of the American immigrant dream.

Her folks were married in Warsaw in 1910, having probably come from Bilgoraj, in the Lublin area. My grandfather, Joseph Weissman, became a naturalized us citizen in 1922. Somewhere along the line he jettisoned Orthodoxy, so that when he and Leah were finally reunited in 1923 after nine years apart, they did not have the foundation upon which to rehabilitate their relationship.[1]

In New York, Joe was attracted to progressive politics. He also dabbled in writing patriotic lyrics for sheet music. Leah, on the other

---

1. Their story shares similarities with Joan Micklin Silver's 1975 Yiddish-English film, *Hester Street*, which starred Carol Kane, about an immigrant couple's struggle over Americanization versus tradition.

hand, remained quintessentially Old World and small-c conservative. She kept her hair covered with a beret following the Orthodox custom for a married woman. In the days before "no fault" divorce in New York, formally ending a marital relationship could be a long, drawn-out business, no matter how estranged the couple, so it was only in 1939, the year of the New York World's Fair in Queens, that Joseph and Leah were finally no longer man and wife.

When my mother was in her teens, Joe was living in the back of his threadbare shoe repair shop on Hegeman Avenue in Brooklyn's East New York neighborhood, where he slept on a cot behind a curtain. Yvette would come by subway from time to time to help tidy the place for him. He was remembered as an amiable fellow, obsessed with politics, and Leah's acculturated Brooklyn cousins nearby seemed to be more sympathetic to "Uncle Joe" than to their own Aunt, occasionally bringing him some home-cooked food to eat in the store.

Like many immigrant Jews, Joe madly adored President Franklin D. Roosevelt, once standing in line from 5 a.m. to catch a glimpse of his hero during a presidential appearance at Ebbets Field, where the Brooklyn Dodgers baseball team played.

Joseph Weissman's passions were progressive politics and Franklin D. Roosevelt

During the 1940s, my mother – by then in her twenties – would dutifully translate Joe's Yiddish poetry (composed to support the Allied effort in World War II and in homage to FDR) into English and then have it professionally typeset and reproduced in a photographer's studio.

Joe also volunteered for the doomed Adlai Stevenson campaign during the 1952 presidential race. I would have loved to meet Joe and understand him better. I may have inherited, DNA-like, my fascination with politics from him. Was he also interested in Zionism? All I know is that in 1953, Joe donated the equipment of his failed shoe repair shop to an outfit called Material for Israel, which helped smuggle weapons to the underground Hagana movement during the War of Independence.

But I never got to know my grandfather; in 1961, when I was seven years old, he wound up in the Harlem Valley State Hospital in Dutchess County, New York, suffering from some kind of breakdown or perhaps the onset of dementia. He died four years later, on May 18, 1965, in that same hospital. He was 78.

When I was a boy, my mother took me to the hospital just once. I have no recollection of the actual visit – I was probably only allowed in the waiting area. On the journey back from Dutchess to the city, I vividly recall that the headlights of our Shortline Bus failed. I can picture the driver steering in the dark by shining a flashlight out his side window, and I remember a thump. We'd hit a tree.

Did this happen as I remember it? A recent article in *The New York Review of Books* about early memories by the 80-year-old neurologist and memoirist Oliver Sacks, got me thinking. "All of us 'transfer' experiences to some extent," writes Sacks, "and at times we are not sure whether an experience was something we were told or read about, even dreamed about, or something that actually happened to us."[2] Indeed, Sacks writes, "It is startling to realize that some of

---

2. "Speak Memory," *New York Review of Books*, February 21, 2013.

our most cherished memories may never have happened – or may have happened to someone else."

Not long after my grandfather died, a man named Frank Duran showed up on our doorstep in the projects. Turned out that he too had been a patient at Valley State, and wanted us to have a gift: a portrait he had done of my grandfather. The painting shows a dignified, professorial, white-haired man in a jacket and tie, sporting a goatee. It hangs in my study as I write these words.

In contrast to Joe, my grandmother, *Bubbe* Leah, was a ubiquitous presence in my early life. In her prime, she worked indefatigably, off the books, schlepping buckets of water and clearing up wet towels at the Russian & Turkish Baths – *shvitzes* in Yiddish – on East 10th Street between First Avenue and Avenue A, and (if I'm not mistaken) also as a *mikve* lady at a ritual bath for women. It's probably from her that I inherited my love for a good *shvitz*.

Leah Weissman wanted a strictly Orthodox husband for Yvette

Monday and Thursday mornings found her, likely the only woman, in the upstairs ladies' gallery of the Anshei Meseritz Synagogue on Sixth Street near First Avenue, listening attentively to the weekday Torah reading. Otherwise, her well-worn Book of Psalms was an ever-present appendage.

I sometimes try to imagine what New York was like when my mother was growing up. I know that when Yvette was in her second or third year of high school – this would have been at the height of the Great Depression when Fiorello H. La Guardia, an insurgent Republican, had just been elected New York City's mayor – Leah asked her to drop out and start working full-time. That is how my mother came to take a sewing machine operator's job – first in a cousin's factory, and later at Brue & Schneider on West 21st Street. Those years spent inhaling textile process dust were probably a major contributing factor years later in her developing chronic debilitating asthma and diminished lung capacity.

I don't know a whole lot about my mother's social life before she met my father, only that she had her fair share of suitors, and that none of them were ever *frum* enough for Leah. Throughout the Second World War, she'd maintained a running postcard correspondence with George Zimmerman, an Army Air Corps Master Sergeant from Manhattan's West Side. Yvette was an avid picture postcard collector, and George devotedly sent her hundreds of cards from all the interesting places the air corps took him. She must have cherished his "Till We Meet Again" Valentine's Day Card, which I found among her papers. George also gave Yvette a Plexiglas picture frame decorated with two .50 caliber bullets, which became part of my inheritance.

Did George and Yvette stay in touch during the six or seven post-war years until she met and married my father? My highly organized mother kept a great deal of correspondence – but, curiously, not a scrap of paper from that period. Whatever Yvette's feelings for George, I doubt Leah would have accepted him as a son-in-law.

Leah didn't want Yvette to marry a man who would merely keep kosher and not work on Saturdays; she wanted someone who was altogether more European and strictly Orthodox in his devotion.

The pressure exerted by Leah for her to marry must have been overwhelming, and Yvette's biological clock was, after all, ticking. She was well into her thirties when Anshel, somewhat her junior, came into her life.[3]

Yvette photographed by her not-religious-enough suitor George Zimmerman

---

3. The fact is that I don't know for sure how old Yvette was. Her age was fudged to meet the needs of official paperwork (lowered or raised depending on the contingencies of the moment). She herself didn't know. She could have been anywhere from 34 to 39. Anshel was most likely 30, though whether his official birthday is his true birthday I do not know.

Chapter 9

"What's It All Been For, Really?"

There is more than a trace of reddish-blond remaining in Raymond Schwartz's full head of wavy combed hair. With his tidily trimmed beard, the short, fit, 70-year-old retired teacher exudes a friendly yet authoritative air. I can visualize that he would have had little trouble holding the attention of any high-school English class.

Taking a sip of herbal tea while studiously ignoring the biscuits the waitress has brought to our table, Ray unfolds his story, beginning matter-of-factly with the assertion that socially, he was a very slow developer. "By my late twenties and early thirties I had, for some reason, still never considered starting a family. I am sorry about that now – obviously," he says. "Sometimes, I imagine what it might be like having a son that is grown up; someone I would like just because of who he is, not only because he's my son, but because he's such a nice guy. I've got friends who have that, and I can say that they have something I will never know – *I will never know* – and that makes me a little sad, no question.

"Yet when I think about it, having kids is a selfish act. Do we have them for *them*, or do we have them for us? The idea of guiding kids so that they don't make the same mistakes we made is not a good enough reason. And it would not work anyway. Everyone has to make their own mistakes."

He had opportunities. Ray had plenty of casual romantic relationships, but for most of his life the last thing he wanted was to make the kind of commitment children entailed. He attributes the choices he's avoided making to his upbringing, which included a domineering mother and a reticent father. Ray's mother came from Poland to Saskatchewan in 1928 to marry his father, who was already in Canada, having arrived in 1902 as a toddler with his family. Together his parents opened a grocery store in Winnipeg – and it stayed open seven days a week, closing only for Rosh HaShana and Yom Kippur.

Like a number of the childless men I spoke to for this book, Ray had a complicated relationship with his father. "Let's face it – we are what our parents make us, to a certain extent. Mom was very dominant – she'd put my father down a lot. Even as a child, when you see this, it registers, you know something is wrong. So I suppose that one reason I didn't marry for so long is that I never wanted to be in a situation where I was being put down. Because I felt so sorry for my father.

"My mother would have done anything for me. She certainly had a great influence, there is no question. Her approval was very important. She was a fine woman – don't get me wrong – but the way she treated my father affected the way I related to women." Then, as if reading my thoughts, he adds, "But how long can you go on blaming a parent for something like that? I mean, at some point you have to take responsibility."

Though both his parents passed away years ago, Ray still seems distressed by the stymied relationship he had with his father. "We never went to a ballgame, or to the park, or on hikes. I think we went to the movies – once. I don't know if he knew how to be a great father. He wasn't the kind of guy who would tell you things you could live by."

Ray has an older sister, now divorced, whom he describes as having been emotionally absent in raising her children, behavior he attributes to their own upbringing.

Ten years after his father died, Ray happened to be in Israel and found himself talking about him openly, maybe for the first time, and vividly remembers bursting into tears. "I recalled this image of my father in the grocery store. He would weigh stuff on the scale, and my mother would hover around and look over his shoulder to make sure he was doing the right thing – charging the right amount, that he wasn't undercharging. I looked at that and, as a kid, I remember feeling so sorry for him. I always felt that I never gave him *koved* – respect – and I should have because he was a decent, nice man," he says, softly.

Like some of the other men I spoke with, Ray is an admitted waverer: "If I am going to buy milk or bananas, I dither – one bag, or two? One kilo, or two? I can obsess over the silliest things. I never owned a home – well, I did for two weeks, and then I immediately sold it."

After he left home he lingered in bachelorhood. His one commitment was to teaching English – literature, language, Shakespeare – in Winnipeg and Toronto.

"I once lived for two and a half years with a woman who had two children, and that didn't turn out to be a good experience at all. I like kids. I thought, I'm a teacher and dealing with kids comes naturally to me, but this was different. My girlfriend's children were 14 and 12, boys, the older one was into drugs. Those kids needed her undivided attention; their mother should probably not have allowed me into her home. That 14-year-old and I didn't get along. They remember me with no fondness."

When Ray's mother died in 1994, he had an epiphany: Life is short. Teaching was all right, but did he want to be in this job ten years on? And if he didn't, why should he continue to spend the next ten years doing it? So he quit, taking early retirement at 53 and spending more time traveling.

The Talmud tells us that you can improve your luck by changing your location (Rosh HaShana 16b). For Ray, the turning point came when he moved to Israel from Canada in 2010. "Something changed in me. I've had this late realization that the path we are on does not have to be the path we continue on. Look at me now. I recently married. My wife and I are buying an apartment. You have no idea how, in times past, such a commitment would have petrified me. With Julia, I just knew it was the right thing. I was serene with my decision."

I asked Ray if he'd ever felt stigmatized for being childless. "No. But I sure felt stigmatized for not being married."

After he moved to Israel he began volunteering with troubled religious teenagers – kids who'd gone off the *derekh,* or traditional path – and derived great satisfaction from teaching them English. But ask Ray whether life has some transcendent purpose, and he'll tell you, "When we're dead, we're dead. This is it. This is all we've got. Death is hard to face. There is a party going on, and I am going to be asked to leave one day. The nothingness of it…," he trails off.

Then, hedging his bets like the practiced ditherer he is, he allows, "I could be proven wrong…. Anyway, you get to a stage in your life and you say, 'What's it all been for, really? What do I leave behind?' So, yes, I have regrets about not having children. It's a real problem. I'm not Shakespeare. I'm not Churchill. I'm not [Jonas] Salk. Churchill had kids and grandkids – but that isn't why he's well known and remembered. No!"

In other words, children may guarantee your being remembered – but only temporarily, and only within the family circle.

Taking a final sip of his now cold drink, he says, "I give myself three months of being remembered after I am gone. After that, I won't even be a memory, and I am not kidding myself."

Chapter 10

Who Remembers Plato?

Raymond's point that history doesn't remember Winston Churchill for having fathered five children got me thinking. Neither, *mutatis mutandis*, has it forgotten Hitler, though he had none.

I know some adhere to the trope that childless men don't care about future generations. Even someone as clever as Harvard historian Niall Ferguson denigrated economist John Maynard Keynes, arguing that his ideas reflected lack of concern for future generations because Keynes was childless and homosexual. Though Ferguson later apologized, I suspect his remarks reflect a common prejudice. Writing in *The American Conservative*, Daniel McCarthy points out that Keynes had already been criticized in a 1946 obituary, when Joseph Schumpeter wrote that the latter's childlessness begot a "philosophy of life that was essentially a short-run philosophy."

Generally, though, being childless has had no influence on how historians have ranked, say, US presidents James Buchanan (a lifelong bachelor), Warren Harding (who died leaving a scandal-ridden administration), or George Washington (an American legend). In contrast, John Tyler, father to fifteen, is not considered a great president – outside the boudoir.

I find myself especially drawn to discovering which Jewish historical figures and contemporary personalities are childless. It's not a case of misery loves company. Though there is a voyeuristic element. I'm in the same shoes as...the prophet Jeremiah, for instance.

The more I fixate on the question, the more childless men seem to emerge from the woodwork. The nineteenth-century philanthropist Moses Montefiore; British prime minister Benjamin Disraeli; *ḥaredi* luminary Rabbi Abraham Yishayahu Karelitz the Ḥazon Ish; child psychologist Dr. Lee Salk; Jewish Theological Seminary Talmud professor Saul Lieberman; and the Lubliner Rav, Meir Shapiro, popularizer of the *Daf Yomi*[1] system of Talmud study.

Once the hunt begins there's no stopping me, especially since friends send me their contributions. So add the spiritual mentor of Gush Emunim, the movement to settle Judea, Samaria, and Gaza, Rav Tzvi Yehuda Kook; the Ribnitzer Rebbe, Chaim Zanvil Abramowitz, renowned for his miracle-making; British chief rabbi Israel Brodie, the first chief rabbi to be knighted; the previously mentioned Lubavitcher Rebbe, Rabbi Menachem Mendel Schneerson, considered the Messiah by his followers; the Satmar Rebbe, Joel Teitelbaum, who came from Sighet, close to the Pater's Spinka; New York City mayor Ed Koch; musician Vladimir Horowitz; *Painted Bird* author Jerzy Kosinski; *Thirteenth Tribe* author Arthur Koestler; and the inimitable Philip Roth, though he did, of course, father the legendary characters Alexander Portnoy and Nathan Zuckerman.

There's Allan Bloom, the political philosopher and Chicago University classicist, who wryly commented in *Love and Friendship* that "children are a great blessing and joy, but one must forget an awful lot in order to see eternity in them." Political theorist Leo Strauss – one of Bloom's mentors – is a special case. He attributed

---

1. A seven-and-a-half-year cycle in which people – individually, with partners, or in groups – learn a folio page (two facing pages) of the Babylonian Talmud each day.

great value to children in marriage. Strauss adopted the son of the widow he married, and later became in loco parentis to a niece whose parents were killed in an accident. Interestingly, Strauss penned the intellectually dense *Spinoza's Critique of Religion*, the fifteenth-century Dutch philosopher being yet another childless Jewish man.

And that's without thinking too much about childless women. If they made it into my consciousness, they were most likely strong-willed and assertive – women who didn't let themselves be stigmatized. I'm thinking of Ayn Rand, the radical free market icon and polemicist; Bertha Pappenheim, who, as Anna O, was the founding patient of psychoanalysis, and went on to establish the League of Jewish Women, a feminist movement in Germany devoted to social justice; Emma Goldmann, the anarchist political activist, philosopher, and writer; and Hannah Arendt, who famously, and controversially, wrote about Adolf Eichmann's role in the Holocaust, originating the term "the banality of evil," and penning the weighty political philosophy classic *The Origins of Totalitarianism*.

Maybe characters of this caliber, women or men, can get away with their pride intact, their childlessness notwithstanding – but what about the rest of us?

It turns out that most Americans would disagree with the proposition that people without children "lead empty lives," or even that the presence of children is "very important" to a good marriage.[2] Of course, Americans appreciate that a vibrant society needs children, but most don't seem to hold it against anyone, individually, if they don't have any. Furthermore, studies have shown that the happiness of people in Western societies is only loosely correlated to whether they have offspring. In our hierarchy of non-material needs, "loving and being loved" is the key condition for human happiness, while "the presence of children in the household appears not to be associated with higher life satisfaction," according to Columbia University's *World Happiness Report*.

2. "Childlessness Up Among All Women; Down Among Women with Advanced Degrees," *Pew Research*, June 25, 2010.

So putting it all together, children do not automatically guarantee a large historical footprint, or high personal status, or happiness. What seems to matter a great deal to people, whether they have children or not, is being in an enduring relationship with a partner, having genuine friends, strong family ties, and (for many) a relationship with God.[3]

German novelist Hans Fallada reminds us in *Alone in Berlin* that every man dies alone. And yet when you are facing debilitating illness and worried that you will be leaving your partner alone, that's when I think the absence of children, and faith, is most frightening; when you're "scared to death" you need religion most. As Alain de Botton has argued in *Religion for Atheists*, religion offers an inherently valuable framework for living that the secular would be wise to emulate.

I had a professor in my sophomore year at Brooklyn College who shocked me – for all my bravado, I was, after all, a sheltered yeshiva boy – with the emphatic declaration that ancient man created God when sentient beings first gathered around the lifeless remains of a loved one. There and then they decided that there *had* to be deeper meaning to life than birth and struggle for survival, followed by an early, likely violent, death. The professor asserted, reasonably enough, that the funeral rite was probably the earliest religious ceremony.[4]

There is a Hebrew equivalent for "Here lies," found on most Jewish tombstones along with another acronym that stands for, "May his or her soul be bound up in the bond of eternal life." On the face of it, of course, the inscription is an oxymoron, for life is finite, while eternity, by definition, is not. Eternity is perpetual; life is fixed. Perhaps the verse is a supplication rather than an assertion.

---

3. "The New Science of Happiness," *Time*, June 9, 2005. The article also cites a survey of American women which found that they derive happiness from sex, socializing, relaxing, praying, meditating, eating, exercising, and watching TV. Spending time with their children ranked considerably lower on the happiness-producing scale. Also worth a look is the First World Happiness Report Launched at the United Nations, April 2, 2012.
4. In sacred history, the first death reported in the Bible is a murder, a fratricide (Gen. 4:8).

We have a need to remember the dead; and I, for one, find comfort in the thought that the souls – the essence or consciousness – of our loved ones live on in some fashion in the cosmos. At the same time, it saddens me that when I am gone, the earthly memory of my mother will fade with me. That thought troubles me more than the temporariness of my own transient mark on this earth.

Children can best be counted upon to remember their parents with unique fealty. Once the children pass on, however, that intensity of connection is lost – instantly. Not even the most devoted grandchildren can pick up the slack. Isn't it humbling to ponder that though they may live on at the DNA level, the identities, accomplishments, and failures of nearly all the humans who ever walked the face of the earth have been erased for posterity? Yet wanting to be remembered in perpetuity – whether through children, the recitation of Kaddish, or leaving the world a better place – never mind that it's unrealistic, impractical, even irrational, helps infuse our lives with meaning.

As a childless man I particularly like the "leaving the world a better place" approach. Take retired IRS agent Anne Scheiber, who lived thriftily and alone on Manhattan's West Side playing the stock market until she died at age 101. She never married or had children and left the bulk of her $22 million estate to Yeshiva University. It was a windfall for the institution, which remarkably had had no previous contact with Scheiber. It turned out that, long retired, she had parlayed $5,000 in savings into a vast fortune. Her lawyer and stockbroker, the only people who apparently knew much about her, said her gift was intended to "help Jewish women battle the kind of discrimination she felt she had encountered during twenty-three years with the IRS."

Upon announcement of the endowment, Rabbi Norman Lamm, at the time chancellor of Yeshiva University, said in gratitude: "The Torah says that he who teaches his friend's son Torah, it is as if he gave birth to him. Here's a woman who for a hundred and one years was childless, and now becomes a mother to a whole community. Not only now, but for generations to come."

Now contrast Scheiber's inspiring story to the sensational, maddening, and, ultimately, disheartening account of childless Holocaust survivor, widower and real estate mogul Roman Blum, who died, age 97, in 2013, leaving his considerable estate to the New York State tax authorities. If reports are to be believed, he was born in Chełm, Poland – which will only contribute to the rich reservoir of folk tales about the "Wise Men of Chelm." As *The New York Times* put it, "Perhaps the greatest mystery surrounding Mr. Blum is why a successful developer, who built hundreds of houses around Staten Island and left behind an estate valued at almost $40 million, would die without a will."

Maybe it's best not to read too much into the fact that Blum died intestate because, after all, 50 percent of Americans *with* children don't at present have a will. Sure, it's possible Blum was making a statement that would bolster Niall Ferguson's notion about childless men not caring about the future. On the other hand, just as is the case with Pablo Picasso (four children) and Howard Hughes (nine children), we may never know why Blum didn't leave a will.

But when a childless man dies without a will – even if he doesn't have a substantial estate – he is probably making a statement, even if it's subconscious, about how he thought about his legacy.

To my mind, Scheiber is a far more uplifting model for a meaningful childless life. She follows in the footsteps of Henrietta Szold, another mother to generations of young Jewish women and men. The life of this Baltimore-born daughter of a rabbi famously took a turn when her love for a younger man was unrequited. In due course, she channeled her energies into helping found the largest Zionist membership organization in American history, Hadassah. It developed into an indispensable health provider, still caring for the people of metropolitan Jerusalem, Jews and Arabs alike, more than six decades after Szold's death.[5] It is where Lisa and I did our IVF treatments.

---

5. I'd be delinquent if I didn't note that the hospital (which has several campuses) has fallen on hard times. Funding for the facilities from the US-based Hadassah organization has dramatically fallen, and Bernard Madoff's thievery left an apparently irreparable $90 million hole. Since Hadassah is not a public hospital, funding from the state insurance programs is limited to reimbursements.

Lisa's father, David, died after a brief illness in the summer of 2013. It was a heavy blow to the entire family and she was determined to say Kaddish, even though that role in traditionalist circles is typically filled by sons. My father-in-law, though open-minded, belonged to an Orthodox synagogue for many years in London and then in Herzliya, and had three daughters. Lisa decided that she would take it upon herself to recite the daily memorial prayer with a *minyan* (quorum). It just so happens that the shul conveniently located around the corner from our place in Jerusalem is Orthodox. Even though she was one of only two women at the 6:30 a.m. service, the men on the other side of the partition made her feel welcome in their "club." In some places, Orthodoxy is evolving right before our eyes. And to that I say: Amen.

Lisa's determination recalls Henrietta Szold's heartfelt reply to her friend, Haym Peretz, when he offered to say Kaddish for her mother. "The Kaddish means to me that the survivor publicly and markedly manifests his wish and intention to assume the relation to the Jewish community which his parent had, and that so the chain of tradition remains unbroken from generation to generation, each adding its own link. You can do that for the generations of your family," said Szold.

"I must do that for the generations of my family. I believe that the elimination of women from such duties was never intended by our law and custom – women were freed from positive duties when they could not perform them, but not when they could. It was never intended that, if they could perform them, their performance of them should not be considered as valuable and valid as when one of the male sex performed them. And of the Kaddish I feel sure this is particularly true."[6]

And while we're on the subject of leaving a legacy, I can think of no better role model than Nechama Leibowitz, for her audacious independence and creativity. A master teacher, she helped reinvigorate Bible study among a generation of Israelis – religious

---

6. "Henrietta Szold on Saying Kaddish," *Jewish Women's Archive*, http://jwa.org/teach/golearn/feb06.

and non-observant alike. Though a professor of education, Leibowitz branched out into informal grassroots teaching. She started out by personally disseminating mimeographed study sheets she'd written, aimed at illuminating the basic meaning of the weekly Torah portion. Unlike the writers of most weekly study sheets, Leibowitz wasn't pushing homilies or political manifestos in the guise of Torah. Her talent was in synthesizing and anthologizing the work of classic Bible commentators, and she filled this role in an authoritative and accessible style. Moreover, this childless widow opened her cramped Jerusalem apartment to anyone who wanted to study with her. Classically Orthodox, Leibowitz was nonetheless a trailblazer for other learned women who wanted to teach Torah. Over time, her no-frills *parasha* sheets were published in book form and ultimately translated into English.[7]

Could anyone persuasively argue that the lives of the men and women recalled here lacked meaning because of the absence of biological children? Whatever their failings – political, theological, even moral – it cannot be said that these individuals did not lead lives of substance. Could this be what the author, philosopher, and childless man Francis Bacon (1561–1626) had in mind when he controversially wrote: "And surely a man shall see the noblest works and foundations have proceeded from childless men; which have sought to express the images of their minds, where those of their bodies have failed. So the care of posterity is most in them that have no posterity."

Take the childless ancient Greek philosopher Plato, for example, who devoted himself to inquiring about the best course of life, by positing that each of us needs to pursue excellence and virtue for a life of meaning. Naturally, parents can add meaning to their own lives by imbuing their children with virtue and, in so doing, bolster their own upright behavior. Those of us without children can't be virtuous "for the children." Our challenge is to find the inner strength to pursue the best course of life even when we are not obliged to set

---

7. Her elder brother was the controversial jeremiad and philosopher Yeshayahu Leibowitz.

an example. In this regard, Hillel, one of the founders of the Rabbinic movement in the first century of the Common Era, famously summed up virtue in Jewish terms: "That which is hateful to thee, do not do to thy neighbor. This is the whole doctrine. The rest is commentary. Now go forth and learn."

We don't need to be superstars to be virtuous. Men and women without children are under no requirement to lead extraordinary, Plato-like lives in order to make them meaningful. Like anyone else, "all" we need to do is strive to live every day with grace, morality, and equilibrium.

Chapter 11

Kaddish'l

One of the cruelest, most unforgiving words in the Hebrew language has got to be *akar*, the word for "childless man" – literally "uprooted," as in utterly uprooted from life, community, and the World to Come. It's not any more palatable when used in the feminine, *akara*, also translated as "barren."

Sherry Blumberg poignantly captures the word's capacity to sting in her 1986 essay in *Sh'ma: A Journal of Jewish Ideas*.[1] Going through the Jewish sources, Blumberg describes how, as a traditionalist, she found herself asking, "What did I do?" She writes:

> If my reading of the *peshat*[2] is correct, then I am being punished. I become angry at God; I scream, cry and find little

---

1. "Some Jews Among Us – *Akarah*," *Sh'ma*, December 12, 1986.
2. The plain or contextual meaning of canon (as distinct from *remez*, its allegoric meaning; *derash*, how the Midrash interprets the text; and *sod*, the esoteric or hidden meaning of the text).

solace in prayer. People who do not want children and who abuse children have them so easily; my husband and I, who would love and cherish a child, cannot.

While I was writing this book, Lisa told me something she had never told me before, describing an incident that took place when we were visiting the home of good friends of ours, blessed with four precocious children, shortly after we halted IVF treatments. The kids attend religious elementary schools, imbibing, like mother's milk, the biblical stories of the matriarchs and patriarchs. Whenever we visit, they invariably surround Lisa, vying for her attention and the thoughtfully chosen gifts she's earmarked for each child. On one such occasion – I must have been off chatting with our hosts – a thought popped into the mind and out of the mouth of the seven-year-old girl.

Lisa did not have any children, right? That's correct, she replied.

"So that makes you an *akara!*" the little girl burst out triumphantly.

Her big sister, sensing intuitively that there was something wounding in the way the word had been hurled, or perhaps catching a glimpse of the hurt on Lisa's face, cut off the discussion in the way only big sisters can, by returning the children's attention to their gifts.

"It was as if I had had a knife thrust into my stomach," Lisa told me, all these years later.

Of course, the little girl meant no harm, but she had unwittingly expressed a long-standing motif within Judaism. Consider, for example, that a sage without progeny – no matter his wisdom – was ineligible to serve on the Sanhedrin, the Jewish High Court which functioned until the fifth century (Sanhedrin 36b). Religious commentators, including the Tosafot and Maimonides (in his *Mishna Torah*), rationalized this on the grounds that a man who is not a father is "devoid of paternal tenderness." Surely, even in the twelfth century, it was plain that some men are tenderhearted and others are not, irrespective of whether or not they're fathers.

In many Orthodox synagogues, even today, a prerequisite for being a *baal tefilla*, or communal prayer leader on the High Holy Days, is being a married man with children. Frankly, I can live with not being on the Sanhedrin or a High Holy Day cantor. My own egalitarian shul doesn't even encourage me to lead Shabbat services simply because I have Diaspora-sounding Ashkenazi pronunciation, and I've gotten over that.

However, some of the ideas put forth by the Talmud appear morally obtuse. For example, Rabbi Joshua the son of Levi raises the proposition that, "A man who is childless is accounted as dead, for it is written [quoting the Matriarch Rachel], 'Give me children, or else I am dead.' And it was taught: Four are accounted as dead: A poor man, a leper, a blind person, and one who is childless" (Nedarim 64b).

Now, I appreciate that the Babylonian Talmud's sixty-three tractates are not necessarily to be taken as authoritative. They've been described as disjointed lecture notes from graduate level courses given between the third and seventh centuries. The Talmud's values, enduring as they may be, are after all anchored in a particular time and culture, and understanding them requires not literalism but painstaking exegesis and an appreciation of the Talmud's unique syntax.[3]

Such nuances, however, are lost on the masses. The stigma remains.

Not all that long ago, some rabbis were known to encourage married couples to break up within ten years if they had not managed to produce any offspring. In pre-Holocaust Warsaw, for example, the Radzyminer Rebbe divorced his wife of thirty years because she did not produce progeny. The younger woman he married gave him a son, who in short order inherited the Radzyminer mantle. This only son, however, was murdered by the Nazis in 1942, leaving no direct descendant to recite the Kaddish memorial prayer for either of his parents.

Walk through Me'a She'arim in Jerusalem, Kiryas Yoel in upstate New York, or Gateshead in northern England – all hasidic enclaves where Yiddish is still the lingua franca – and you just might overhear a *frum* (religious) mother referring to her angelic little boy as "my *kaddish'l*."

---

3. Besides, the opinion of any rabbi in the Talmud is not necessarily authoritative.

That's because the moment a son is born, his parents have what amounts to memorial-prayer insurance for the period of "after 120 years," the hoped-for lifespan in traditional Judaism. This man-child can be counted upon to recite the Kaddish prayer for the dead – linking God, eternity, and children. "He who is survived by a son devoted to Torah is as though he had not died," one rabbi in Genesis Rabba (49:4) posits. On the other hand, an entry in the Zohar, also on Genesis (90b), states: "He who has not a son is called childless."

Rationalists may understand the Kaddish as actually designed to bring comfort to survivors and as a way to publicly commit to carry on the deceased's legacy.[4] But rationalism gets you only so far.

What happens if you die without a *kaddish'l*? You could cover yourself by paying an enterprising charity to assign someone, perhaps a rabbinical student, to say Kaddish for your soul during the first eleven months after you pass on – and, for an additional premium, in "perpetuity" on the annual *yahrzeit* anniversary of your death.

Of course, all this assumes that death for the childless is the same as for everybody else (and you don't subscribe to the view that the childless are like the walking dead). Yet there is space within Jewish tradition to conclude, as did Rabbi Joshua the son of Levi, that even the Afterlife is denied to the childless.

Look at it this way: Children are a guarantor of eternal life, writes Étan Levine, professor emeritus of Biblical Studies at the University of Haifa in his *Marital Relations in Ancient Judaism*. Following this logic and citing the Talmud's Bava Batra (116a), Levine observes that while King David was said to have "slept with his fathers" in life-everlasting, his army commander Joab, who died without siring a son, was just plain "dead."

It's a churlish idea picked over by other talmudic discussants (*inter alia* Yevamot 55a) and later medieval kabbalists, who presumed that no offspring equals no heaven, no hell – leaving only one way out: reincarnation and another stab at procreation. This reincarnation

---

4. Joseph Hertz, *Affirmations of Judaism* (London: Oxford University Press, 1927), p. 153.

notion is a post-biblical construct that entered Judaism through mystical teachings, in particular the Zohar, the idea being that multiple lifetimes provide our souls with the opportunity to make up for a presumed failure – in this instance, childlessness.

Embracing the myth that those of us without children will find ourselves on a fast track to remedial reincarnation gives me little comfort, though it does tell me something about the mindset of its credulous enthusiasts.

Chapter 12

Spinka on the East River

Anshel and Yvette were married in March 1952, at the Astoria Mansion catering hall on East Fourth Street on the Lower East Side. My mother handled the arrangements and no doubt footed the bill – after all, she was the one with a regular paycheck. What followed were probably their best years. They honeymooned at Niagara Falls, holidayed at Papa Klein's pastoral upstate farm, and sent each other birthday and Valentine's Day cards. He called her "honey," she called him "dearest Alan."

They were living with Leah in her 108 St. Mark's Place railroad flat with its coal stove in the kitchen and a sink that also served as the bathtub. One of my own early memories of the place was noticing the vertical pipes delivering steam heating up from a newly installed basement boiler. In Jerusalem, Lisa sometimes uses Leah's old undersized coal shovel for gardening.

Yvette, ever organized, straightaway filed an application for a modern apartment at the nearby Jacob Riis Housing Projects, which

The best years: the Pater with "Papa Klein" circa 1952

had been erected between the East River and Avenue D in 1949. My parents were placed on a three-year waiting list.

As with many a failing marriage, each spouse expected to change the other. Anshel had inexorably gravitated to the *stiebel* of Shmuel Tzvi Horovitz, known as Reb Hershele, a Spinka hasidic master newly (albeit temporarily) resident on the Lower East Side. It was here that he began reconsidering his choice of coming to America and wondering what living in the Holy Land might be like. Yvette, while valuing Jewish tradition, wanted their married life to realize the American dream. They could be observant Jews and refined Americans. So she took him in July 1953 for his first – no doubt only – library card.

Under Reb Hershele's sway, Anshel prevailed upon Yvette to replace her dainty kerchief with a *sheitel* (wig) in the manner of strictly Orthodox married women. Coming home every morning from *davening*, Anshel would regurgitate Hershele's *musar* or homily preaching humility and, above all else, dread of sin. The Pater was reverting to his Old World Spinka religious roots. Leah had called it right.

On a chilly and rainy Election Day 1954, my mother took a green and yellow Checker taxi – alone – to Mount Sinai Hospital on Fifth Avenue, where I was born by Caesarian section the next day. She had been through several traumatic miscarriages by the time that I – a sickly infant, by all accounts – made my appearance.

Alan and Yvette in 1952: three years later he was gone

Not long ago, the Pater told me candidly, earnestly, eerily, that my birth was a preternatural occurrence: "You are here because of the *kavana*" – spiritual mindset – "with which I recited the twenty-fourth Psalm." What did he mean in attributing my birth to a *ness*, or miracle? Was he implying some kind of psycho-sexual problem?

"I am not a man like other men. I am not a strong man," he hinted. Hence his reliance on the Psalm, which reads: "He who has clean hands and a pure heart; he who strives not after vanity and swears not deceitfully, he will receive a blessing from the Lord." And yes, he told me, the arrivals of each of his daughters from his second wife were no less wondrous.

Of course, the Pater is inscrutable. Some ultra-Orthodox men supposedly adhere to benighted regulations codified in the sixteenth century governing sexual relations, which urge having Torah-related thoughts during intercourse and otherwise avoiding "levity." So, who knows?

The first time he walked out with just the clothes on his back was when I was five months old. The Pater made his way from the Lower East Side first to the Rockland County ultra-Orthodox enclave of New Square, and from there on to Montreal, where, with the help of the Tosher Rebbe, he found an American Hasid to vouch for him so that he could obtain a duplicate US passport (I assume my mother had custody of his original one). Then it was back to New York City and the West Side steamship terminals.

On April 27, 1955, a Western Union Telegram arrived at 108 St. Mark's Place: "Left For Israel 5 p.m. Alan." He had booked himself into a third-class cabin aboard the legendary *Queen Mary*, bound for Haifa. And he wrote practically every day of the crossing.

> *I know I did a foolish thing by not telling you the exact time when I leave for Israel but your actions decided me to do so when I saw that you hide the bank book from me and you was talking that you can even take me to court. When I heard that I decided that the whole trip is in danger if I am going to tell you the exact time of my departure. More details next letter. Regards to every-body and to Elelele [Yiddish for Elliot] to momma [Leah] and to Rabbi Halpern, Love Alan.*

In a letter dated Friday April 29 written on posh *Queen Mary* stationery, the Pater sounds almost giddy:

> *Dear Evette, The 3rd day on the ship the weather is fair. The waiters are friendly, the people who clean and take care of the rooms are friendly and courteous – after all I am an American tourist – they will get a nice tip. But they don't know that I haven't money to spare. Tomorrow is Shabbos and I hope you and the baby and mama have a gutten Shabbos, Alan.*

In his mind he must have convinced himself that he was scouting out a future, better life for both of them – and me – in the Holy Land.

Arriving in Israel, he found refuge for two and a half months at Kibbutz Ḥafetz Ḥaim near Gedera, located south and inland from Tel Aviv. His postcards home described the holy sites he'd visited and implored Yvette to join him. It would be a snap to find a place to live as well as work on one of the farming *moshavim* (settlements), he promised my mother. If she rebuffed him, however, he raised the specter of divorce. Incidentally, he'd add, could she send some spending money?

Before he knew it, his tourist visa was about to expire. But he'd made his point. It was time to return to New York – so, naturally, he wrote Yvette asking her to buy him a return ticket as soon as possible.

As chance would have it, there were no imminent ship crossings to New York. Probably for the first time, certainly not for the last time, Yvette turned to "the cousins." This was an era when relations were also friends, when immigrant kin felt a strong bond with each other and socialized together. The cousins pooled their resources and raised a staggering $491.60 for a one-way El Al ticket from Tel Aviv to New York. I'm guessing the cousins figured that keeping the marriage going was the best choice of available options. Yvette's health was on the skids; during Anshel's absence she had been hospitalized for what may have been stress-induced asthma and exhaustion.

After he picked up his El Al ticket in Tel Aviv, Anshel wrote another "Dear Evette" letter from a park near the airline's offices. He confessed to being frightened before his first flight, which would most likely have been aboard one of the airline's new Lockheed Constellation propeller planes.

The way the Pater remembers it, the only reason he came back was because Yvette promised that it was just a matter of time before they'd all sail together as a family to Israel for good. But in a June 1955 letter my mother was unequivocal: Given their limited financial resources, "the baby's health," her responsibilities to Leah and her strong disinclination for working on a farm, she would not risk a move to Israel.

The choice was his.

Had he not seen her letter when, on July 15, 1955, Anshel wrote, "Dear Wife, I am coming back from Israel not because I am giving up on the idea of settling in Israel. But with the idea we should go settle in Israel within two to three years. Alan"?

They were broadcasting on different frequencies.

Yvette was also being practical; the Pater was a dreamer. She'd been struggling economically all her life; now, though, she owned a refrigerator and telephone and had health care. In 1955, most Israelis did not have the appliances even working-class New Yorkers took for granted, and even money couldn't necessarily buy hard-to-obtain antibiotics.

On his return to Manhattan, the Pater brought along two small canvas bags containing Holy Land earth and stashed them underneath the living room *seforim shank* (bookshelves) where his religious tomes were shelved. They were still there when he left for good.

For the Pater, the desire to live in Israel had nothing to do with the political Zionism that brought me to the country decades later.[1] As he saw it, there are *mitzvot*, sacred commandments, that can only be fulfilled in the Holy Land. And living in an all-Jewish cocoon, after everything he'd been through, promised a sense of serenity he surely craved. Still more strategically, the Pater knew that people buried in *Eretz Yisrael*, the Land of Israel, would be first to be resurrected with the coming of the Messiah.

Before he left, my father and I must have shared some good times, though I have only the blurriest memories of them. On Saturday nights after *Havdala*, the Pater would light a candle – as if to extend the sanctity of Shabbat – and read to me in Yiddish from the spellbinding *Shivḥei HaBesht*, an early collection of legends about the founder of Hasidism, the Baal Shem Tov, and his disciples. I still have the book. I still light a candle after *Havdala* – though in memory of my mother.

Afterwards, he'd tune the radio to WEVD – "the station that speaks your language" – and listen to Rabbi Mordechai Pinchas Teitz read a *blatt Gemara* (two-sided page of Talmud) in Yiddish. Teitz

---

1. As I mentioned, my mother and I first visited Israel in August 1976. At the time it didn't even occur to me to make contact with my father – not that I would have known how. The same is true for several subsequent trips I made.

would sign off after his Talmud program with *a gute nacht mama*, wishing his mother a good night.

There are other memories. It's summertime, when religious families from the Lower East Side band together for vacations in ramshackle bungalows in the upstate New York Catskill Mountains. Such compounds once dotted the Monticello and Liberty area. Husbands and fathers would come up on Thursday night or Friday morning for *Shabbos*, and return to their jobs in the city late Sunday.

I am with my father at the colony's gender-segregated swimming hole. Bearded men and boys with *payes* (sidelocks) are frolicking in the murky water, floating on tire inner tubes. The Pater, in good spirits, is holding my hand tightly, cajoling me to enter the lake with him. In another memory fragment, though, he is already in the water.

Either way, I am really frightened.

In another memory, it is a morning before Pesaḥ, and my mother has asked Anshel to take me to the playground while she makes final preparations for the Seder. We probably went to the park alongside the FDR Drive and played catch. That, and the time I sleepily walked into the toilet during the night to find him urinating – take that, Dr. Freud – almost exhaust my paternal memories.

But here is another. We are in Williamsburg, Brooklyn, in the waiting room of Satmar Grand Rabbi Joel Teitelbaum.[2] Ushered into the rebbe's office for a blessing, I remember being awed by the wood-paneled walls. The rebbe pinches my cheek, exchanges some words with the Pater, and we leave with a *kidesh-becher*, a wine goblet used for sacramental purposes. I still use it every Shabbat.

What I remember most about my father was his resentment of the wicked pleasure I took in watching television. After numbingly drawn-out days in yeshiva, I longed to plop down on the floor directly in front of our black-and-white set. This was before remotes, and I wanted to be close enough to adjust the volume and change the channels (there were five at the time). The Pater viewed television

---

2. The childless hasidic Grand Rebbe.

as a diabolical appliance which snatched me away from my religious studies and distanced me from God's will. He was right on that score. It was and it did.

I was, maybe, seven years old when he once came home – unexpectedly, I guess – to catch me mesmerized in front of the television. Enraged, he made as though he was about to remove his belt and chased me around the dining table. I never did figure out how we even came to own a television. It must have been one of the many points of contention between my parents.

Long after he was gone, I used the cash proceeds of my bar-mitzva loot to buy a brand new black-and-white Philco Ford television; still no remote. Today, Lisa likes to point out that there are more TV sets than people in our apartment. Maybe I'm overcompensating.

Coaxed and coached by Yvette, Alan passed a 1956 civil service exam for a US Post Office job and began work the following year. By 1960, he was a mail handler (he didn't deliver mail, just sorted and organized it), earning a respectable $4,535 annually – just $1,000 below the national median income of the time.

Anshel's unhappiness in America, though, was undiminished. His principled refusal, as a Sabbath observer, to do a late Friday shift caused him grief with his post office supervisors. Meanwhile, Yvette, ever resourceful, had become active in the neighborhood Republican Party clubhouse, campaigning for its candidates, including Richard Nixon. In fact – and I'm not making this up – I was the only six-year-old sporting a Nixon button in first grade at Yeshiva Chasam Sofer. Anyway, Yvette was getting the hang of working the system. Using her connections with the club's captain, Mr. Weinberger, she was able to get Anshel permanently exempted from late Friday and Saturday shift-work.[3]

---

3. I don't know why my mother – contrary to the overwhelming Jewish consensus – became a Republican. Perhaps it was simply a function of the fact that she had access to Mr. Weinberger and not to some Democratic politician. In those days you could be a New Dealer and a Republican just like Fiorello La Guardia. The Democratic Party was still in the hands of corrupt Tammany Hall bosses who'd managed to elect their candidate, Robert Wagner, as New York City mayor.

But there was not much she could do in response to his *kvetching* that the mail sacks he was expected to lift were too heavy. Or about his being hassled by his non-Jewish co-workers. My dad didn't fit in.

Then, early one morning in April 1963, when I was eight, he left for good. What specifically precipitated this second and final exit, I don't know.

For my mother it was the humiliating final straw.

Even now, I can remember my palpable relief that the Pater was gone. After all, his absence meant I could watch *Romper Room*, *The Sandy Becker Show*, and *The Sonny Fox Show* unhindered; home life would be more tranquil. With a hat tip to Oedipus, I recall, as I mentioned, sitting proudly at the head of the table, leading that Passover Seder at the age of eight. When it came time to read the Four Questions, I did that, too, since I was also the youngest (and the only) boy.

The Pater found initial refuge in Brooklyn's Crown Heights neighborhood, not among its Lubavitcher denizens but among a Spinka sect led by Rebbe Yaakov Yosef Weiss. He sent Yvette an artful letter proposing a "visit" and providing a Brooklyn phone number where he could be reached. Suspecting – correctly – that he was buying time before making a run to Israel, my mother found a lawyer and preemptively filed suit in Domestic Relations Court demanding child support.

At a joint court appearance, the hearing judge ordered routine psychological tests for both my parents. My father must have shown signs of a man unraveling. He told the judge that my mother had hired a menacing black man to follow him around. That got the Pater placed under brief psychiatric observation at Bellevue Hospital. Upon discharge, he did a runner, essentially replicating his earlier getaway to Israel, but this time taking care to send nominal amounts of child support – a money order for $10, for example – to placate my mother and stall the authorities until he was safely out of the country.

At last, in early 1964, the Pater arrived in Israel and did something he apparently hadn't done the first time. He tracked down his brother, Chaim Yitzhak, whom he had not seen since 1941. A year earlier, Chaim Yitzhak had written the Pater asking for financial help and lamenting that they had not seen each other for so long. He had included a portrait of himself wearing a dark double-breasted suit and tie. The brothers bore a striking resemblance to one another, though Chaim's handsome face seemed fuller, his hair stylishly combed. And, more significantly, Chaim had become an *apikoros* (heretic). Just as the Holocaust had only strengthened the Pater's belief in God, it had had the opposite effect on his brother.

The letter Chaim had sent assumed that Anshel was raking it in at the post office, and that Tante Golda and her husband, Naftali, were making good money from their candy store on Sherriff Street in the shadow of the Williamsburg Bridge.[4] Upon receiving Chaim's letter, Yvette decided to have her Israeli cousins, the Liss family, evaluate firsthand just how precarious Chaim's financial circumstances were. If things were as bad as his letter purported, maybe Alan and Yvette could scrape together some money to help Chaim purchase that refrigerator he hankered after.

Helen Liss (my grandmother's niece) and her daughter, Miriam, made the then arduous bus journey from Raanana to the Ezra Zion neighborhood of Rishon LeZion and dutifully produced a detailed account. Chaim was making a better than tolerable living at Israel's Government Printing Office. He'd married an altogether decent, energetic woman of Hungarian origin with two studious and personable daughters. The couple had no children of their own, Helen noted. In other words, my uncle was a childless man.

In the end, Alan and Yvette sent a gift toward the new refrigerator.

Helen Liss added, "Alan's brother resembles him a bit as to facial features. His wife said that she pushes him to everything; because his philosophy is '*vus men hot is genug*' [what we have is enough]."

(Five decades later, I mention something about my job to my father. He takes a perfunctory interest in order to set the stage for what he really wants to tell me: The purpose of life is not work, but to prepare for the World to Come. A person should work the absolute minimum necessary and not squander his energies on the temporal.)

---

4. Urban renewal later forced them to move the store to 181 East Broadway.

Anshel and Chaim were finally – probably unsentimentally – reunited. They put their heads together. Anshel wrote his ex-employers at the US Post Office from his brother's house, asking for his back and severance pay. Once in hand, these funds provided him with some financial wiggle-room. Next, Chaim helped him land a job with the Ritual Slaughterers Association at the Carmel Market in Tel Aviv. The work involved affixing *kashrut* bands around animal parts certifying that they were kosher.

As the Pater was settling in, back in New York my mother received a letter from the Israeli Consulate informing her that "Mr. Jager" had applied to change his status from tourist to new immigrant. The Israelis wanted to know: "Did Mrs. Jager plan to join him in Israel?" Was this standard bureaucratic procedure, or was it the Pater's way of using a third party to let my mother know that, despite everything, he'd welcome her joining him?

Her reply was curt: She was not interested one way or the other "in Mr. Jager's status." Take that.

In halakha, Jewish religious law, only the husband can initiate *get* or divorce proceedings; and if he wants, he can refuse to do so, and leave his wife – and himself – in indefinite marital limbo. The Pater still recalled the assurances from Heizler the matchmaker that Yvette had money. Hadn't she agreed to send funds for Chaim's fridge? More than that, not long before he fled, my father had purchased a deluxe set of tefillin – on a layaway plan.[5] When Yvette found out about the costly purchase, she paid off the invoice in a single payment. That certainly established beyond any doubt in the Pater's mind that she had some cash stashed away somewhere.

Now Anshel hit upon the idea of withholding the *get* until Yvette offered him some kind of pecuniary inducement. That, however, got him nowhere, and he began to waver. One late afternoon in August 1964, he showed up unexpectedly at the Liss home on Moshav Givat Ḥen near Raanana just as the family was planning to leave for a

---

5. The Pater had reserved the set which was held by the scribe as he made payments on a regular schedule. Under this system, the buyer only gets the item after all payments are completed.

wedding. Sporting a "bushy black beard" and a "vacant look," as my cousin Miriam recounted in an aerogramme to my mother, the Pater told Yvette's family that he was prepared to grant her a *get* without financial compensation and would even sign an affidavit committing to child support – should he ever return to the US.

Miriam added that her family had the impression there was something not quite right with Alan. Despite his pledge to their family, it took international rabbinic intervention, including by the Lower East Side's revered Rabbi Moshe Feinstein – and the threat of physical intimidation by Miriam's gentle-giant of a brother, Paul – before Alan grudgingly, and with no quid pro quo, granted Yvette a divorce in the fall of 1965.

I tagged along when my mother went to plead for the intervention of Rabbi Feinstein, a meeting that would likely have been arranged for her by Rabbi Halpern, the family's religious *consigliere* and Feinstein's neighbor. That encounter has stayed with me ever since. It was mid-afternoon. Feinstein himself came to the door. We must have disturbed him – studying, sleeping, in the toilet – because he seemed terribly put upon. And he remained out of sorts the entire visit.[6]

I've scanned some of the hagiographies written about "Rav Moshe," but my conclusion remains that the encounter in his apartment on Grand Street was no aberration. During the five years I would later spend at Mesiftha Tiffereth Jerusalem (MTJ) high school, where Rabbi Feinstein served as the head *Rosh Yeshiva*, he showed himself to be a quintessential Lithuanian non-hasidic ultra-Orthodox leader – stern, preoccupied, and frosty.[7]

---

6. There were many warm and open-hearted clergymen in Rabbi Feinstein's orbit, especially in the study hall *beis hamedrish* – from the *shammes* or sexton, Rabbi Schiff, a real *mensch* who taught me how to lead weekday morning services in Rabbi Feinstein's presence, to the *Rosh Yeshiva's* saintly son-in-law, Rav Moshe Schisgal, who exuded only warmth.

7. Rabbi Feinstein was thrust into the ultra-Orthodox spotlight with the death in 1962 of Rabbi Aharon Kotler of the Lakewood, NJ yeshiva. These were old-world rabbis who promulgated insular, uncompromising, non-Zionist European Judaism in post-World War II America. It could well be that Feinstein found his

At the time of the Feinstein encounter, I was still enrolled at the insularly Orthodox Yeshiva Chasam Sofer.[8] My elementary and junior-high-school rabbis ranged from the kindhearted Rabbi Pivovits, who never raised a hand against us and spoke a splendid, delightfully memorable Lithuanian Yiddish, to Rabbi Unger, a volatile *Galicianer*, whose mood swings left us on continuous edge.

Every so often my mother had to go through the indignity of pleading before a Chasam Sofer committee for reduced tuition. She'd threaten, half-heartedly and unconvincingly, to pull me out of yeshiva and enroll me in public school if we weren't granted a scholarship. Both out of compassion and because the last thing Chasam Sofer wanted on its conscience was to shove an innocent, yarmulke-wearing boy into an inner city, co-ed, *goyishe* Lower East Side municipal school, the yeshiva directors invariably agreed to bill Yvette only a nominal monthly charge to keep me in yeshiva.

While, academically, particularly in terms of secular studies, my Chasam Sofer years were pretty much a black hole – though I did hone my skills as a Yiddish mimic – I have mostly fond memories of the place. One of my favorite characters in the madcap cast was the atypically cheerful, red-bearded principal, Rabbi Friedman, a roly-poly fellow with a British accent. He'd bounce into our otherwise dreary Talmud lessons every so often for a spot quiz, interjecting his trademark phrase, "What say we have a *faher*?"[9]

---

public role stressful. The ultra-Orthodox world made demands on its foremost talmudic decisor. As a boy I must have been unnerved by the fact that the great sage was also an imperfect human being with foibles and vulnerabilities.

8. The school, established by Rabbi Shmuel Ehrenfeld, was named after a founder of ultra-Orthodox Judaism, the Chasam Sofer (1762–1839). He was a passionate opponent of Reform Judaism which had come upon the scene in the nineteenth century. His motto was "'new' is forbidden by the Torah." By the time I arrived, the school had merged with Shlomo Kluger, and in the early 1960s, moved from Houston Street to Broome Street. It is presently located in Brooklyn.

9. An oral examination on our understanding of Talmud. In both my yeshivot, little effort was made to contextualize or make the Talmud accessible. We were simply expected to know who said what (in Aramaic) and regurgitate the obtuse commentaries.

My mother didn't spin the Pater's departure to win me to her side. That was unnecessary. In any dispute with my father, I instinctively sided with her. I would be well into middle age before I even tried to understand his motivations. At the time, my father's absence left no void. His obsessive religious fervor was a source of tension and unhappiness. Religious practice was not an important element in his life – it was the *only* thing that mattered; there was no space for anything else.

As I witnessed my mother struggle to take care of her elderly mother, put food on the table, keep a roof over our heads, be a *balabusta* (homemaker) of the first order, and maintain me in yeshiva, I became ever more attached to her. I knew she wasn't perfect. She was older than the mothers of other boys my age. I sensed that other boys didn't have the kind of shared lives with their moms that I had with mine. She was prone to sporadic bouts of melancholia and nothing unnerved me more than to see her miserable. After a dreadful asthma attack, or when she was in excruciating pain from bursitis in her shoulder that made it impossible for her to lift her hand, or after one of her terrifying unstoppable nosebleeds, we'd come back from the hospital emergency room and she'd climb dejectedly into bed. She'd wail in Yiddish to *Gotenu* (dear God) that she just could not take the pain and loneliness any more. What had she done to deserve such a life? On one of those occasions, when she was so distraught that she was near the end of her rope, I heard her lash out at the Pater. She wanted him to feel her pain. I wanted that, too.

We were in a mutually dependent relationship. I was her companion. Two only children bound by love, blood, and hardship.

She showed only perfunctory interest in remarrying; prospects were presented, but none of the life-long bachelors or widowers swept her off her feet. I suppose she was emotionally spent. As a teenager, consequently, though I wanted to push the boundaries of independence, I held myself in check knowing that if I went too far, too soon, if I behaved toward her the way other "normal" boys growing up in "ordinary" families treated their mothers, she'd be wounded.

Weirdly and out of the blue, in July 1966, when I was 11, Anshel sent Yvette a letter, using his brother's place as a return address and offering my mother one absolutely, positively, last chance to reconsider.

> *Dear Mrs. Jager, I admit that I made a mistake [when] I left the home. I am longing for the child. But two wrongs does not make one right. If you would not be stubborn and come here we can re-marry again. Let me know. I will not bother looking for somebody else.... Sincerely, A. Jager.*

What went through my mother's mind when she read that, God only knows. I doubt she bothered to reply. Under Jewish religious law, I recently learned, a couple is not precluded from remarrying each other. Indeed, in some hasidic circles it is considered meritorious for a man "to take back his divorced wife."

Another letter arrived in September before the High Holy Days.

> *Yechaved Channah [Yvette's Hebrew name], since it is a custom before Yom Kippur to ask forgiveness therefore I ask from you to forget if I made maybe against you any accusations and after [illegible] can make a mistake, let's forgive each other. A Happy New Year. Also, I ask from Elliot forgiveness and wish him a Happy New Year.*

Though he was geographically where he wanted to be, my Pater must have been terribly tormented, frightfully lonely, guilt-ridden, feeling he had no way out. No wonder, then, that he sought comfort by moving ever deeper into a particularly superstitious stream of ultra-Orthodoxy.

It must have been sometime before Israel's 1967 Six Day War that the Pater made peace with himself – as far as he was able – and put the American phase of his life behind him. Like any number of deadbeat dads, he covered his tracks, changed his surname, and opened a PO Box in Jaffa for all future communications to anyone connected with his previous life. Though we didn't know it, he'd settled in Benei Berak, in the metropolitan Tel Aviv area, where his Spinka sect had a solid base.

My guess is that it was around 1970 when the elders of the community matched him with Devora, a twice-widowed, iron-willed Persian-born woman who already had two children from two separate, now deceased, husbands. Marriages between Farsi-speaking Persians and Yiddish-speaking Ashkenazi Hasidim are rare, but given that neither seemed to have a winning track record, allowances were made.

Anshel's reasoning in agreeing to the match, he would tell me in old age, was that Devora – given her own baggage – was unlikely to want to divorce him; nor would she be excessively demanding in the marital sphere. Self-effacing, he didn't mind a domineering wife so long as she shared his religious sensibilities. My father and Devora did produce my half-sisters Sheindel and Esti. And, partly with the help of a government subsidy and support from the community, the couple was able to place a security deposit on the humble rental flat where the girls were raised and where I would one day be hosted.

Chapter 13

A Cosmos Insensate

Tall, slightly stooped, with a posh accent, unkempt white hair, eyeglasses halfway down his nose, and sporting the de rigueur tweed jacket, Benjamin George, 71, strikes me as having been sent from central casting for the role of British intellectual. Indeed, he only recently retired from a tenured position as a professor of anthropology at an English university. We rendezvous outside the Union Square branch of Barnes and Noble in Manhattan and stroll over to a nearby café to talk about childlessness. Benjamin describes himself as an unreconstructed European, London-born, old-school Zionist – read Labor – who finds himself living in Brooklyn Heights only "because of an American lady who is now my wife."

It was not until sometime in his fifties that he realized he would not be having any children. His wife was never interested in them. He hadn't married earlier; probably, he thinks, because he was brought up in a splintered, dysfunctional family, though the immediate cause was a love triangle he got caught up in when he was in his thirties. "I became involved with two women – who, at different times, I would have wanted to marry, and who at different times would have wanted to marry me – but neither relationship led to marriage. It was rather traumatic. It stopped me from marrying for a very long time."

Like just about every childless man I interviewed, he says that he really likes children and has never made any secret to his friends of how much he regrets not having any. Now he greatly regrets not having grandchildren.

Benjamin had a complicated relationship with his parents. He was the first of his generation born and brought up in England, his mother and grandfather having escaped Germany before the Nazis came to power. His father wasn't Jewish and his parents divorced when he was very young. Benjamin was brought up by his mother, who came from a secular German Jewish family.

He spent very little time with his father during his childhood because of lingering hostilities between his parents. While his mother eventually remarried and moved to America with Benjamin's younger sister, Benjamin stayed in England to attend university. It was only at that point, when he was 17, that he began to see more of his father, who was now his closest relative in England. They developed what he describes as a very good relationship, but by then his father could not influence him deeply. Benjamin's father died when he was relatively young, in 1971; his mother lived until 2006.

"I had a very difficult relationship with my mother," Benjamin tells me. "She was a very horrible woman – a really nasty person – whereas my father, I think, was rather a nice person. I didn't know him as a son normally knows his father, but we got on very well. Both my sister and I detested my mother." Coming from what he thought of at the time as a "broken home," Benjamin did not want to risk marrying anyone he wasn't sure he'd stay with. He tells me he could have married and had children – "if one or two things had been just slightly different."

He and his wife met in 1973 but didn't become a couple until the 1980s, and didn't marry until the '90s. "I didn't think of marrying her, partly because she is not Jewish, and partly because she did not want to have children. So it was only sometime in my fifties – when it became clear to me that the age for having children had really passed, unless something very special happened – that I was ready to make a real commitment to her," he says.

I asked Benjamin if, as a Jewish man, he ever felt stigmatized for being childless. He wasn't that kind of Jewish man, he tells me. "When I was growing up we went to shul only three times a year, and didn't keep kosher. In adulthood, I lived in a cosmopolitan, secular, academic milieu and gave no thought to Judaism's stereotypes about childless men."

In the West, he reflects, there is a contradiction between self-fulfillment and having children. "Children demand tremendous effort and sacrifice. I find it interesting that people who are most fond of children have the least children. The non-Orthodox Jewish population is one example, and the Italians are another. The Italians have the lowest birthrate in Europe and they are really fond of children."

Does he worry what will happen to him as he gets older? "We are in a very strange world," he replies. "My wife is looking after her mother, who is a comparatively healthy ninety-six year old. The situation in our society of people in their seventies looking after people in their nineties – we are not really built biologically for that. But I can't say the question of who will look after us weighs heavily on me. One reason it doesn't is that you see how stressful it is for the children. However attached they are to their parents, it is a great relief when the parent finally dies. So it's true there won't be someone to help me with my tax returns when I'm eighty-nine, but, on the other hand, I'm glad I won't be messing up someone's life."

As a self-declared non-believer, does he think there are spiritual implications of being childless? Benjamin ponders the remains of his coffee before replying. "I consider the universe deeply, deeply mysterious. The idea that there is someone out there who cares about me individually and who is weighing up my deeds has no resonance for me. In the sense that I don't believe in a Jewish God, I am an atheist.

"There might be a religion out there – perhaps pantheism – that I might have a little more sympathy for. My outlook on the world is totally determined by what science tells us about the universe – which is enormous beyond all our imagining. It has a beginning in time and, apparently, an end in time – at least in its present form. It is quite conceivable to me that we will never understand the universe.

"I certainly have a strong sense of the mystery of the world. But the idea that this or that religion has got the right answers seems to me absurd. If anybody gets an answer, it is going to be people like physicists. Paradoxically, though, religion derives from the same impulse as science – to make sense of the universe around us, and the very strong feeling that what we see is not what we've got. Science has shown this to be very much the case. The nature of material objects is so different from what our senses and intuition tell us.

"What *is* true is that my life is impoverished. My life would be happier or richer if I had children – probably. Of course, anyone who has children is also hostage to fortune." To emphasize the point he adds, "Had I had children but couldn't do the kind of intellectual work I like doing – let's say I'd been forced to make a living in some well-paid but intellectually undemanding job like being a stockbroker, and I'd been very successful in bringing up a brood of children – I think I would have been more frustrated than I am now, where I haven't had children, but have had a rather satisfying intellectual life."

"So life is full of meaning for you without children?" I ask. "I don't think life has a purpose. I don't think life has a meaning. These are constructs we ourselves endow it with, and the meaning we endow life with depends on factors ranging from biology to personality."

The professor wants to show me a book that he feels will better make this point, so we stroll back to Barnes and Noble. On the way, he acknowledges that his idea of the world is a very stark one. I tell him he is not the only childless man to tell me that.

Back in the store he adroitly tracks down the book he wanted to show me. It's a collection of poems by Matthew Arnold (1822–1888), whose work confronted the crumbling of Christian faith under the weight of nineteenth-century scientific discoveries, foremost among them evolution. "Look at his poem 'Dover Beach,' which begins: 'The sea is calm to-night. The tide is full, the moon lies fair.'" Benjamin then reads me this excerpt:

The Sea of Faith
Was once, too, at the full, and round earth's shore
Lay like the folds of a bright girdle furled.
But now I only hear
Its melancholy, long, withdrawing roar,
Retreating, to the breath
Of the night-wind, down the vast edges drear
And naked shingles of the world.

"The 'Sea of Faith' represents the universe," Benjamin explains. "What this means to me is that you trudge around. You do your best. You try to be decent. You can't even describe the sea as cruel – it is unfeeling. But somehow you can't help anthropomorphizing it."

Chapter 14

Welfare Cases

There never was any secret stash of cash. When the Pater vanished, so did his bi-weekly Post Office paycheck. Yvette's cousins stepped in to fill the breach, covering the rent and paying for groceries. But that couldn't continue. And so, in the late 1960s, to my mother's mortification – and mine – we became "welfare cases." By applying for what was then called "income maintenance," we joined close to a million other New Yorkers, mostly Blacks and Puerto Ricans, on the dole. Of course, there were tens of thousands of other poor Jews living in New York, but they were mostly the left-behind elderly, not people like us.

One reason Yvette had been so insistent that the Pater provide child support was that city social workers had warned her that an application for welfare could be jeopardized if she divorced without paternal child support arrangements firmly in place.

By now, Yvette had her hands full. Her fiercely proud and headstrong mother, Leah, was becoming increasingly confused, something our family physician, Dr. Reich, attributed to a hardening of the arteries. Bubbe, as I called her, had moved in with us and could sit for hours on end near the living room window, reciting Psalms. With increasing frequency, when the door was not secured, she'd wander off. Once, in the middle of the night, my mother woke up startled to see a black man in our living room. He was a kind-hearted neighbor who'd been returning from his night-shift job when he came upon Bubbe and brought her back to us.

One of my most distressing memories dates back to when I was, maybe, 11 years old and home alone with Bubbe. She must have been agitated, and in trying to get her to sit down, I pushed her. She missed the chair and landed on the floor. For the life of me, I can't remember if that's when she broke her hip, or if it happened on another occasion. Either way, I have always blamed myself.

Bubbe was hospitalized in an open ward at the old Bellevue Hospital, a municipal facility on First Avenue. Besides the crowded conditions, hospital smells, and moaning patients, there was incessant construction hammering coming from a drill auger pounding away just below her bedside window. Our visits were nerve-racking and I broke out in an itchy rash that came and went for months. Leah died from surgical complications on October 27, 1965.

So in that one *annus horribilis*, 1965, Yvette lost both her parents, divorced, found herself indigent and on welfare, and was left to raise me – a bratty, demanding, clinging boy. Her magnanimous cousins – the Guttermans, Sebolskys, Steinkritzs, Penzers, Bazers, Weisses, and Starks – continued to pitch in, paying for the funerals of both Leah and Joseph, including chapel services, rabbis' fees, headstones, and the burial plots in New Jersey.

And yet, with all that and the welfare checks, our expenses were still not fully covered. Obviously, the city couldn't make allowances for the higher cost of kosher food and *glatt* kosher meat, so Yvette sought part-time jobs, off the books. In her spare time she sewed and sold aprons to neighbors and friends. She also found work at Sam's Snack Shop across from my elementary school on Broome Street. I had anyway been a loyal patron of Sam's greasy, salted French fries, which he sold in small brown paper bags, and which I preferred to the flavorless macaroni and USDA-surplus canned peas that were the mainstays of our school lunches.

There wasn't all that much money in the French fries business, so Yvette started working as a saleslady at Al Friedman's on Clinton Street, selling leather and suede coats. The job required evening hours, and I used to throw tantrums when I came home from school to a dark and empty apartment. So rather than have me crankily call the store every few minutes to *nudnik* Al about when my mother would be coming home, he'd let me hang around the store, keeping me occupied with sweeping the floor. He even let me help decorate the display windows.

I had always thought of my mother as a rock, but the stresses of life exacerbated her asthma attacks, which became more frequent, more debilitating, and sporadically life-threatening. When Mom got a really bad, middle-of-the-night attack, we'd dial "O" for operator and plead urgently for an ambulance to take us – in a harrowing, vertigo-inducing, siren-piercing race – to Bellevue Hospital's emergency room. Then there was the seemingly interminable wait until a medical resident finally injected epinephrine adrenaline into Yvette's arm. Only then could we both breathe easier. Around then, Yvette discovered that a strong dose of percolated black coffee could help keep her breathing passages open. It's another reason why I've always considered real, strong-roast coffee to be the nectar of the gods.

With my grandmother's death, and as I became marginally more self-sufficient, my mother had greater flexibility in the kinds of jobs she could apply for. Yvette had a professional phone manner, could compose excellent business letters, was highly organized, knew her grammar, had good arithmetic, and fine penmanship. But without that Washington Irving HS diploma and no touch-typing, her options were limited.

Her struggles to get us off welfare weren't easy, and there was no shortage of setbacks. Like the time she landed a promising file-clerk's job at the classy Metropolitan Insurance Company on Madison Avenue, not having revealed that as a Sabbath observer, she'd have to leave early on Fridays. Chances are she would not have gotten past the interview had she been forthright; still, Yvette was devastated when she was dismissed during her first week.

Eventually, though, she found part-time work that gave her a lot of personal satisfaction. She became a paraprofessional school aide at Manhattan's PS 40, where the principal, Mr. Sklar, recognizing her abilities, assigned her to the library. It was only because the job didn't guarantee sufficient hours year-round that she sat for and passed a civil service exam to become a clerk at the New York Health Department.[1] That job finally delivered security and benefits, though little joy.

---

1. Being a Sabbath observer was now much less of a problem. For starters, the department was historically a "Jewish agency" in the sense that NYPD was Irish and Sanitation was Italian. Jewish employees could arrange to leave early on Fridays and make up the time during the week, or have their early departures charged to annual leave hours. Ironically, an officious, non-observant Jewish time-keeping clerk occasionally did complain that Yvette left "too early" on Fridays, but in every instance her Catholic supervisor accepted that she needed time to prepare for the Sabbath, and not merely arrive just in the nick of time for candle-lighting.

Chapter 15

Casualty of War

A t 75, Simon Black is a man who has clearly aged well. Good-looking, tanned, and decked out in well-tailored business casual, he was returning to Paris when we met up in a relatively quiet spot of Tel Aviv's Ben-Gurion Airport. A retired scientist and entrepreneur, Simon years ago sold the biomedical company he founded and divides his time mostly between homes in France and Switzerland.

Born in London to German Jewish refugees who'd arrived in England in 1937, Simon was separated from his parents just prior to the beginning of the devastating London Blitz – when, in 1940, he was dispatched for his own safety to America.[1] His mother and father were concerned that if England were to be invaded by the Nazis, Jews of German origin would top the list of Jews to be done away with.[2]

---

1. Germany's bombing campaign lasted from August 1940 to May 1941 and killed 40,000 civilians, destroying a million homes.
2. By 1940 much of Europe (excluding the Soviet sphere) was in Hitler's hands. Forced deportations to concentrated ghettos had begun; Himmler ordered Jews

Many families – and not only Jewish families – decided they wanted to get their children there. Simon's parents had family in the States, relatives who had gotten out of Germany with his father's help. "So I was sent off, in August 1940, with an English nanny," he recalls. "My parents, because they had German passports and also because of professional commitments my father had, were unable to leave England." Accompanied by his nanny, he spent four and a half years in America with various members of his family. He was two when he left and six and a half when he returned to England at the end of 1944. Much later, after the breakup of Simon's marriage, he got into therapy, and began to uncover how traumatic this separation had been for him.[3]

Simon then spent five "not entirely happy years" with his parents, who lived in a city in mid-England. In the intervening years, Simon's father had managed to reestablish himself, running a flourishing architectural firm. "By all material standards I had a very comfortable life, and grew up in what was essentially a loving family," he says. "My parents' marriage was intact and I did not want for anything in the context of what was available in postwar England. But my father was a *yekke* of the highest order.[4] And his *yekkish*-ness extended to a totally unnecessary level of discipline that I was subjected to. It wasn't, I suppose, that he didn't love me; he loved me very much, but he was probably unable to show it. He felt that he needed to apply a sort of Prussian discipline to my upbringing, which went completely amiss. It was totally unnecessary.

---

refusing transfer to be put to death. In Poland, Jews were forced to wear yellow stars. However, the meticulously planned mass murder of European Jewry would not begin until 1941, while the systematic and industrial genocide received its official imprimatur only in January 1942. See Walter Laqueur (ed.), *The Holocaust Encyclopedia* (Yale, 2001).

3. Thousands of British city children were evacuated to safer places within the United Kingdom, with some three to four thousand being sent to America and Canada. Transatlantic travel soon became too dangerous because after September-October 1940, the German navy began torpedoing British ships.

4. *Yekke* connotes not only a Jew of German-speaking origin, but also a near-obsessive attention to detail and punctuality.

"I was an extremely sensitive child and the whole thing got screwed up. There was some physical element to it – but I was not a particularly naughty child. Mostly, I felt it, for example, at the dinner table. He was ultra-concerned about table manners. He didn't like children to be too outgoing. He wanted to rule the roost in his way. He didn't want any contradiction – he wanted to feel that he was very much in charge of the family home, and this didn't go down at all well with me." Simon collects his thoughts before carrying on. "I had a total breakdown of my self-confidence; I used to burst into tears at very little provocation."

He was enrolled in a Jewish boarding school, which proved a godsend. "It took me away from the immediate influence of my father; it also took me out of provincial England, where there was a not-very-pronounced anti-Semitism – though I did experience some when I was at school." Simon regained his confidence, and went on to study biology at Cambridge. After graduation, he moved to Europe to take a job with a pharmaceutical company, before founding his own firm.

Simon's personal life did not mirror his professional successes, however. While there was no shortage of sexual liaisons, there were no permanent bonds. "I suspect this was because I had, in retrospect, difficulties in forming lasting relationships, particularly with the opposite sex, and that is probably connected to my childhood absence in the States," he says. He had a series of affairs with mainly married women "because, I suppose, unconsciously, it gave me a relationship without the need to make a firm commitment, and thus, probably, avoid the possibility of being hurt and abandoned. And this continued until I was 36."

Then he met and married Eva, a Jewish woman of Polish origin, the child of Holocaust survivors. Following their attempts to conceive, without success, the couple saw a number of fertility experts, but during the late '70s and early '80s, IVF techniques were still in their early stages. At one point, Eva had an ectopic pregnancy, in which the fertilized egg becomes implanted outside the womb, usually in the fallopian tube. That led to further gynecological complications, which made it even less likely that she would have a child.

Had his ex-wife been able to have children, he says matter-of-factly, he probably would have "fallen into fatherhood, not having made a conscious decision to have children, but simply because we were married and the marriage was at that point more or less intact. It would have just happened. Looking back, I have to say that at no point in my life did I feel an overwhelming urge to have children."

Simon's assertion forces me to acknowledge – to myself – that I felt much the same, maybe because I did not have the experience of a "normal" family to aspire to, maybe because I feared being a bad father. It was only after I married Lisa and we discovered that we couldn't have children that I began to see childlessness as a void.

The children issue was, it turns out, part of the reason for the breakup of Simon's marriage. "It became an obsession with my ex-wife. As a child of Holocaust survivors this was something of huge importance to her. I took the attitude that, as far as I was concerned, we didn't need to have children to stay married. It was very much her obsession to have children."

Where does all this leave him today, as a childless Jewish man? I ask.

"Judaism is an important part of my life emotionally and culturally. I am nominally observant. I go to a shul on Shabbat when I can manage it."

Simon has been with his current partner, Anna, since his divorce. A non-Jewish German woman, Anna has a grown child from her first marriage. "She was in her mid-forties when we met, and I was in my late forties – the situation presented itself in such a way that I really didn't have to make any decisions about the possibility of wanting children. By then it just wasn't in the cards. Had it been, and had she insisted on children, I don't think we would have stayed together because there was no way I wanted to get into a mixed religious relationship that presumed children."

Although he does not have kids of his own, Simon tells me he has found joy in being a father figure to his three grown nieces – his sister's daughters – who, in the aftermath of their parents' divorce, do not have a very good relationship with their father. "I find a great deal of meaning in my life by being a sort of surrogate father to them, and, indeed, a surrogate grandfather to my sister's nine grandchildren – my great nieces and nephews. I think my nieces are very happy for me to assume the role of grandfather to their children. They are very much part of my life," he says. "We spend most of the Jewish holidays together."

Before he heads off to the airport's business lounge, Simon tells me that he has recently tried to make posthumous peace with his father, and is currently involved in a philanthropic project to "perpetuate my father's Jewish legacy. I've been going through all his archives – he left a very complete collection. As a result, I began to understand much more about the existential concerns that my father experienced with the rise of Nazism. This better understanding of my father's motives in sending me away connected me much more to my origins."

Chapter 16

"Soft Like Butter"

Five days a week, my mother set off for her city job knowing she didn't quite fit in. For starters, New York City in the late 1960s and early 1970s – save for a few select neighborhoods – was a cauldron of palpable racial tension, anti-Semitism, violent assault, and runaway murder rates. Under mayors John Lindsay and Abe Beame, the city was hemorrhaging its tax-base. Streets were dirty; subway commuting was near-Hobbesian. But I understate.

As I look back on those days from my perch in Jerusalem, I ponder the fact that in any single year of the 1970s, more people were slaughtered on the streets of New York City than Israelis killed by Palestinian Arab terror during the entire second intifada.

New York might have been going down the drain, but I was thrilled to have found my first job. My buddy in ninth grade, Chagi Rubin, was ready to hand over his sinecure at Moishe's Bakery on East Broadway. Moishe was an atypically convivial Satmar Hasid, a natural salesman, a guy probably in his late sixties who didn't look a day over seventy-eight. Moishe's didn't do any of its own baking, so I'd show up well before early morning prayer services to unpack and set up the deliveries of breads, rolls, Danish pastries, cakes, and *mehadrin* (stringently) kosher milk before the salesladies and customers arrived. Then I was off to start my school day.

On occasion, I'd get to see Moishe himself behind the counter. With a Cheshire Cat-like smile, he'd cut a piece of day-old marble cake, "*voch ve-pitter*," soft like butter, he'd say, handing it to a customer to sample. From him I learned about the power of suggestion.

In the evenings I'd return to Moishe's to sweep up the crumbs, wipe down the counters, and prepare for the next day. About six weeks into the job, I screwed up my courage and asked Moishe if, maybe, he could pay me. At first I wasn't sure he'd heard because Moishe wore clunky hearing aids in both ears. So, I tried again, at higher volume.

"Of course, why didn't you remind me?" he said, calling me into the back and lowering himself into the easy chair where he took his afternoon *shluf* (nap). He reached into his trouser pocket, whipped out the biggest wad of dollar bills I'd ever seen and began to count off one… two… three…. He must have kept going until he reached, maybe, thirty-six dollars. I was overjoyed.

My really big professional break came in eleventh grade, when Gerald Gartner, who was in the grade below me at MTJ, turned over his job as shipping clerk/messenger boy at Biegeleisen's Hebrew book shop on Division Street. Biegeleisen's supplied school and library books to Jewish day schools around America while also maintaining a strong inventory of specialized sacred books. There wasn't much off-the-street traffic, but savvy collectors – from hasidic rebbes to Japanese philo-Semites – could be spotted scanning the stacks. The store, founded by their father Reb Yaacov, was now managed by brothers Shlomo and Moishe Biegeleisen, Belzer Hasidim.

The brothers trained me to prepare cartons and Jiffy bags for UPS and US Post Office shipment. Whenever an item wasn't in stock, I'd hop on my bicycle and pick up a copy from a neighboring Jewish bookshop or publishing house, which in those days were still all concentrated between the Manhattan and Williamsburg bridges on the Lower East Side.

I got to know my way around the Hebrew Publishing Company on Delancey Street, Ktav on Allen Street, J. Levine on Eldridge Street, Feldheim on East Broadway and Rabinowitz on Canal Street. Each had its own specialization, and I caught glimpses of their owners – men and women who were legends in the Jewish book world. There was Phillip Feldheim, the quintessential *yekke* in his starched white shirt, waistcoat, and sleeve garters, an expensive aromatic cigar always smoldering in his ashtray. What could be more pleasing than the scent of fusty books and pricey cigars? Naturally, Feldheim himself would not deign to deal with me, but instead called for his manager, Reb Tuvia, to *"zee vat the boy from Biegeleisen vonts."* I had a similar relationship with Rabbi Kestel, who managed J. Levine – you never dealt with the top dog and you were better off for it.

The Biegeleisen brothers were fair and decent employers, and I worked for them for three years, well into my freshman year at Brooklyn College.

Though I was now earning pocket money, Yvette carried the real load of keeping us afloat. At work, Mom toiled away in a windowless master file room, which she shared with six other clerks, all Southern-born black women. Except for Numa Watson they all chain-smoked, which exacerbated Yvette's asthma. Fortuitously, we had found a private respiratory specialist recommended by the Biegeleisens, aptly named Dr. Chusid, who was successfully managing Mom's case. And thank God for oral steroids and inhalers, which by then had come into use.

The file room's supervising clerk was craggy, old Miss Mary Chouncey – Yvette gave her the moniker Moms Mabley because of her resemblance to the African-American vaudeville comedienne – though never to her face. Chouncey would emit the occasional anti-Semitic aside, never directed at my mother personally, and matter-of-factly referred to white folks as "crackers" or "whitey." The atmosphere didn't get any better when, in 1973, New York City voters elected the city's first Jewish mayor, Abe Beame, though it was Ed Koch, elected in 1978, who became the lightning rod for unvarnished minority Jew-hatred.

New York's leading African-American weekly paper, *The Amsterdam News*, for instance, ran the same shrill front-page headline for months on end: "Ed Koch Must Resign." Each issue offered new grounds.[1]

But on a one-to-one basis, Yvette's co-workers were collegial. Even Miss Chouncey had a soft side, and a few of the ladies, particularly Miss Polly, Miss Numa, and Theresa X – she'd joined a sect that broke with the racist Nation of Islam – became Yvette's close friends including outside the office. To this day, Lisa and I use a heavy set of dishes that Theresa schlepped by public transportation to Yvette as a house-warming gift.

All the while, Yvette continued to wear her *sheitel*. She never wanted anyone to misconstrue that my father had left us because she was insufficiently observant. Of course, by now hardly anyone even remembered my father, but a principle was at stake. Moreover, and she didn't even need to say it, I knew Yvette wanted me to adhere to an Orthodox lifestyle – and I did, in the main, for her sake. With all that, my mother nurtured an abiding suspicion of religious and political fanaticism.

She was exasperatingly dubious of, and out of step with me about, the hero I had embraced in 1969, Jewish Defense League founder Meir Kahane. I had risen to the lofty height of deputy lower Manhattan coordinator by the time I quit JDL in 1973, not out of any great principle but because of a petty disagreement with the Manhattan coordinator, Gene Singer, who'd also been my mentor. I subsequently tried to make up for my bad behavior to Gene, who genuinely devoted his life to the Jewish people. But it was good that I quit anyway, because JDL evolved from a neighborhood self-defense group and activist Soviet Jewry gadfly to a religiously fanatic and bigoted group called Kach.

---

1. Though he was married to a Jewish woman, the publisher Wilbert Tatum occasionally employed anti-Semitic innuendo and rhetoric. Tatum took control of the paper and tried to walk a fine line, wanting to boost readership which, necessarily, meant scapegoating the Jewish mayor, though in a more genteel manner than the previous owners and other Black newspapers.

Plainly, I had been hankering after a charismatic father figure – obviously, Dr. Freud – and Kahane fit the bill. He was undoubtedly a brilliant tactician, enthralling writer, and often prophetic pundit. While on a 1990 speaking tour, Kahane was assassinated in a New York City hotel by El Sayyid Nosair, a member of Sheikh Omar Abdul-Rahman's terror cell. The Egyptian cleric had ties to the then metastasizing jihadist network, which today is nominally overseen by al-Qaida's Ayman al-Zawahiri. With time, however, I came to see that Kahane himself was deeply troubled, leading his blind followers down a treacherous path.[2] As usual, Yvette had called it right.

Landing a decently paid tenured City job was just one of Yvette's achievements in those years. Around 1967, she pulled off what amounted to a bureaucratic coup. City policy forbade council housing tenants to transfer from one housing project to another. But we were desperate to escape from the hi-rise Jacob Riis projects on Avenue D, where crime was rampant, the elevators reeked of urine, and we were just about the only Jews left.

At the time, we could hardly afford to move into Co-Op Village on Grand Street, a lower-middle-class enclave erected by the International Ladies Garment Workers Union, where our better-off co-religionists lived. Yvette's talent for composing well-argued, supplicatory, yet convincing, letters to *machers* (influential doers), fixers, big shots, and politicians was brought into play. Writing to Mayor John Lindsay, the head of the Housing Authority, and anyone else she could think of, up and down the municipal chain of command, she cited our need to be within "walking distance of a synagogue" as a mitigating circumstance to justify a transfer into the Vladeck Houses on Gouverneur Street.

Why Vladeck? Because they were a comparatively low-crime, low-rise complex, still ethnically and racially integrated. The neighborhood was on the "good," south side of the Williamsburg

---

2. Perhaps the most revealing insight into Kahane's psychological demons can be gleaned from a January 24, 1971 *New York Times Magazine* piece by Michael T. Kaufman, "The Complex Past of Meir Kahane."

Bridge, just a short stroll to the Grand Street co-ops and the core of the remnant Lower East Side Jewish community. She pulled it off about a year before my bar mitzva. I'll never forget the combination of exhaustion and elation we felt after paying the movers and bolting the door of our new home at 38 Gouverneur Street.

There was just one problem: We had no money left to carry us through until payday. Yvette, again swallowing her pride, turned to our benevolent cousins for just one more handout.

Chapter 17

Aerogrammes

We weren't long settled in our Gouverneur Street flat when an envelope from the Pater arrived, forwarded from Avenue D by the us Post Office. It contained, unusually, a copy of a typed letter from the Pater addressed to the FBI – with that addressee crossed out by pen, and overwritten by hand with the words "New York City Police Department." The letter charged that my mother was still trying to physically intimidate him (presumably into providing child support). It was written to alert the NYPD that they should not be taken in by outward appearances: his ex, my mother, was in contact with a criminal underworld. At the bottom of the letter, addressing himself to Yvette, the Pater scribbled a warning that if she persisted in her designs, it would be she, not he, who'd get in trouble with the authorities.

Had he had another run-in with Paul Liss, our *shtarker* (strong), tough-but-big-hearted Israeli cousin? As far as we knew, he hadn't, and his grievance had no basis in reality. We had no idea where the Pater lived. And by now there were no expectations on Yvette's part that he'd pitch in financially – not even for my bar mitzva. We were gobsmacked.

Was he rattling our cage, just to stay part of the picture? The painful truth is that the Pater did care about me – just not in any way that made sense, or that I could reciprocate. He sent occasional aerogrammes – lightweight, pre-stamped, all-in-one-envelope letters – from his mysterious PO box. They tended to arrive in conjunction with the Jewish holidays. He'd also sent a set of tefillin for my bar mitzva, care of Tante Golda, because he didn't have our new Vladeck address. I do not think I deigned to take possession of the set – if I did, I certainly did not, to paraphrase Exodus 13:9, bind them as a sign, or have them close to my heart. They remained in their pouch.

His aerogrammes never told me anything about his life, and never asked about mine – except in connection with my religious life. Under pressure from my mother, I did reply with assurances that I remained devout. Like I said, it was a matter of honor for my mother that I remain Orthodox – as if to show the Pater.

In fact, I had become an ever-more petulant adolescent with little patience for deciphering his illegible mishmash of English, Yiddish, and Hebrew scribble. To the extent that I perused his epistles, they all contained what struck me as the same tiresome, sanctimonious, and disgracefully hypocritical message: that I needed to strive for ever-greater piety. Piety, actually, was not foremost in my mind. Paradoxically, the Pater was sending me his love in the only way he knew; in the only way he could. He was sharing the Kool Aid, albeit from six thousand miles away.

While my theological outlook was hardly formed, ritually I was biding my time, treading water, first at Chasam Sofer and then at Mesiftha Tiffereth Jerusalem. Only allegiance to my mother and the values she cherished, as well as my involvement with Kahane's JDL – which, funnily enough, helped me understand that being Jewish was not only about religion and ritual – kept me in the fold. But that's another story.

When I was just short of my seventeenth birthday, I decided that instead of ignoring or pacifying the Pater, his by now infuriating letters merited a blunt rejoinder. And so when the next one came, I answered with all the teenage wrath I could muster. I blamed him, personally, for my frustrated, messed-up life. I told him it was his fault that I had been left to grow up in a violent, anti-Semitic neighborhood; it was his fault I had no money. I told him that instead of hectoring me about religion, fear of God, and Torah learning, he should send money. We'd use it to get out of our place on Gouverneur Street – which, as fate would have it, was no longer a safe haven.

By some twist of fate, this irate, intemperate, ill-considered letter – the only heartfelt one I had ever written to the Pater in my entire life – came back stamped "Return to Sender Insufficient Postage."

Well, if God wanted to play *that* game…

The Pater soon sensed that he was getting the silent treatment. It was 1972, he'd been gone some nine years, I was now 18. He wrote pleadingly for me not to cut him off. He'd worked on my behalf for my first "9 (sic) years and I think I deserve a letter once a while no matter who is at fault that we cannot all get along." Moreover, he asked me to remain neutral in "the argument" he had with my mother.

Getting no answer he wrote again, making the daft claim that during their breakup my mother had "promised" that if he would "go back to Israel" and "leave her alone," she would not demand money in child support. *Oyfn gonif brent der hittle* (a guilty conscience) – the Pater knew he'd done wrong and was angry at himself and at the situation.

From about 1973, when I was enrolled at Brooklyn College, until the early 1990s, I doubt I stooped to acknowledge, or even retain, any of his correspondence.

And this is how it came to be that the Pater and I did not see or speak to each other for thirty years. I blamed him for not being curious, in the ordinary sense, about my life. By ordinary I mean the simple stuff. He had never heard me go on about Moishe's Bakery, nor *kvetch* about anti-Semitism in New York. We'd never had an intellectual exchange, talked about books, movies, or girls – *rachmana litzlan* (God save us). He didn't even know that I had become an ardent

Zionist. Maybe he would not have approved of political Zionism, but we never debated the topic.[1]

So of course he never heard that my mother and I made our first trip to Israel in 1976, in the afterglow of the euphoria surrounding the Entebbe rescue operation. Would he have believed that to do so we had to borrow our airfare money from a good-hearted Lower East Side neighbor, Lydia Markowitz?

Of course the Pater didn't know that I majored in Judaic Studies at Brooklyn College, or that I went on to graduate school to study politics at New York University. Or that I worked my way through those institutions thanks to various positions I held at the New York City Health Department. Or that my first break with that agency was thanks to Yvette's patronage.

Did he know from Tante Golda that I was briefly married in the 1980s to a Bronx teacher of the blind? That failure of mine was something I didn't necessarily want him to know about. I didn't want him to think I was walking in his footsteps.

---

1. As for my Zionism, I grew up in a non-Zionist, strictly Orthodox milieu. The only outright anti-Zionist I knew personally was my friend Shulem Luzer Rubin, the Sassover Rebbe's son. He'd been on an airplane and visited Israel. He described the Zionist authorities in the way a Satmar sympathizer would, as Hebrew-speaking gentiles grossly insensitive to religious Jews. He told me that the police beat religious Jews in the street. He'd seen it with his own eyes. Later, Israel entered my consciousness during the 1967 Six Day War, when Psalms were recited during expanded afternoon prayers at Yeshiva Chasam Sofer. The Jews of Israel were in mortal danger and the yeshiva's non-Zionist orientation was cast aside. I came home after school and Yvette and I would watch televised war coverage over supper – and therein was born my lifelong habit of watching the news while eating dinner. Israel had now embedded itself in my consciousness. Here were tough Jews who stood up to defend themselves, so unlike the besieged Jews of the Lower East Side. Eventually, my JDL experience, reading Rabbi Kahane's works, and my involvement in the Soviet Jewry movement, initially through Gene Singer, led me to pro-Israel activities and a growing commitment to Zionism. I took an undergraduate degree in Judaic Studies, including a seminar in Zionist intellectual theory by Rabbi Arthur Hertzberg, author of the best introductory essay on Zionist theory ever written. Mother and I visited in 1976 and I knew then Israel was where I wanted to live. When Yvette died in 1997, I wasted no time in emigrating from the US.

Nor did he know about Golda's warming relationship with Yvette. Any misgivings my mother may have had about Golda in the wake of my father's departure had dissipated with the years. Golda was not Anshel's Trojan Horse; except for sending him the occasional handout, she was barely in touch with him.

Save for Golda's urgings – and Yvette's implied consent – there is no way I would have agreed to resume contact with the Pater. He doesn't know that, either. Maybe the biggest thing my Pater doesn't know about me, and never asked, is what I think about God. All he obsesses about is that I have no child.

Chapter 18

Irreversible Fortunes

I don't have kids, in part by planning and in part by grand design," a man named Benny Wald informs me as we settle in to talk. Born in Ottawa and now in his early fifties, Benny seems mild-mannered, with an open, friendly face and just the right amount of self-deprecating humor. Benny is a filmmaker, and he wants his story to unfold like a documentary, to control the pace. He starts by telling me about how, while in his twenties, he eloped with his first wife, Missy. The last thing Benny did before the couple made their getaway to the justice of the peace, was to visit his religious *bubbe* to tell her what he was about to do. Missy wasn't Jewish, which was a big deal to Benny's family, and he felt he owed his grandmother that much. His *bubbe* told him plainly that she was not happy about it, but that she understood that he had to follow his heart.

In their ten years of marriage, Missy never wavered about not wanting children. There were issues stemming from her dysfunctional family history, and soon after she married Benny, she was traumatized by the news that her parents were divorcing. Benny tells me he himself was ambivalent about not having children. "It was a way of not having to deal with the complications of intermarriage." His relationship with Missy ultimately broke up, but not mainly over children. He wants to keep things vague: She was just not happy, and "wanted space." The divorce was amicable, he tells me, and the two remain on cordial terms.

Around the time Benny was going through the break-up, he became director of the Vancouver Jewish film festival. In a way, he says, it was ironic, given that he was not at all affiliated with the Jewish community at the time. A little more than a year into the job, Benny read on an electronic bulletin board that a singer and actress named Abby, a New Yorker, would be visiting Canada for the first time to attend the debut of a film produced by a mutual acquaintance. He gallantly offered to show her around.

"We met at the film festival and spent a week together. As soon as we met, it felt like a permanent relationship. It was instant." They've now been together fifteen years. "She was more spiritual than I was," Benny tells me. "I come from logical, pragmatic stock."

The turning point came when Benny's father died. Suddenly, Benny decided he wanted to start saying Kaddish every morning for his father. He found himself attending a local shul, and becoming more drawn in to religious observance.

"So here is the bone of the meat of my story," says Benny, laying his hands on the table. "When my first wife and I made the decision not to have kids, I had a vasectomy so that she herself would not have to get everything yanked – a far more complicated surgery. But Abby did want children. When we started dating we were both in our early 30s. Losing my father made me realize that without kids I would never enjoy the kind of nurturing relationship I once had. I realized children were more important to me than I had thought.

"So I had a vasectomy reversal – not successfully. Then we started looking into IVF. This was in Canada, where, contrary to what you may imagine about socialized medicine, fertility treatments were not free. Doctors did what's called a post-vasectomy sperm extraction procedure, and my sperm – they were good swimmers, and there were tons of them – were used to fertilize Abby's eggs in a test tube, then implanted in her womb.

"We did a number of rounds of this. Each attempt cost thousands of dollars. But the implantation didn't take. She's taking hormones. It takes a physical toll; it takes a mental toll. It is exhausting; it is frustrating. It is a rollercoaster of emotions. I guess I felt less bad that my vasectomy wasn't the only stumbling block – it wasn't working on her end, either. It became *our* problem."

Abby felt that maybe they had waited too long. But they were not angry at each other. Emotionally, Benny felt in a less vulnerable situation. "I didn't start out wanting children. I had reconciled to not having any. So when the IVF didn't work out, I was able to return to that place and say, 'OK, it didn't happen; we tried, we did our best.'"

But there are moments of profound sadness for them both. The Jewish holidays, so focused on children, are especially difficult. "I come from a big family, where children were always part of the scene. Where it really hits me is when you get people coming up to us – and this happens all the time – saying, 'You know, you guys would have made great parents.' And I walk away thinking, actually they're right.

"We naturally get asked by people who don't know us if we have children. We say it didn't happen for us, and depending on who we are talking to, they may say, 'There is a *berakha* (blessing) or prayer you should recite, a rabbi you should see....'"

At the same time, Benny thinks that people who get their meaning out of life exclusively through their own children are, in a sense, selfish – limiting themselves to passing on a certain kind of wisdom within their own family exclusively. He feels that he has wisdom to pass on more widely, that there is a community he can give to, just like his father before him – even though he has no children. "I think it is much, much harder for Abby."

Their relationship is strong, he tells me, and at this stage they don't talk a lot about infertility. That's partly because, back in Vancouver, they made a very conscious decision to be public about it. In those days there was no place in the city for childless Jewish people to go for emotional support. So they created a network. "All the talking to other people and being open was our therapy."

I ask Benny the question I'm often asked: Why didn't you adopt? "In point of fact, to adopt is rather complicated in Canada. It's expensive. And we'd spent a fortune on fertility treatments. We'd need about the same amount of money to go down the adoption track.

"I am not someone who looks back at my life and says, 'I should have done this, or done that. I should have zigged instead of zagged; I should have taken the elevator on the left, instead of the elevator on the right.'

"But that doesn't mean we don't hurt. Our social circle is mostly people who have kids. So do I feel the loss, for example, on Shabbat, when I am not blessing my children, while the moms and dads around us are blessing theirs? Yeah." Then he adds, "I feel the loss especially when I think there will be no one to say Kaddish."

He would like to think that God understands that he's doing his best. Part of him thinks that to believe in God is actually kind of foolish. The other part feels that not to believe in God is arrogant. "I don't want to be foolish, or arrogant."

Chapter 19

To Be Jewish, Childless, and Gay

There was a time – and it wasn't that long ago – when being a homosexual man, closeted or out, sentenced you ipso facto to a life without children. For most gay males (aside from closeted married dads), bachelorhood, not fatherhood, was what fate had in store. But all that's changed. Today, young gay male couples can fully expect to become parents, and may even stand a better chance of success than straight couples with fertility problems. Any correlation nowadays between childlessness and homosexuality has more to do with choice than providence.

Paradoxically, as homosexuality has become less stigmatized in the West, people have tended to vastly overestimate the percentage of gay people in the population. Gays, like other minorities, tend to congregate within communities, so we get a distorted picture of how prevalent the gay lifestyle is.

Combine that with confusion about who is a homosexual.[1] In the course of their lives, people may experience same-sex attraction, and perhaps eight percent have engaged in some form of same-sex activity. However, "sexual orientation," according to the American Psychological Association, "refers to an enduring pattern of emotional, romantic, and/or sexual attractions to men, women, or both sexes. Sexual orientation also refers to a person's sense of identity based on those attractions, related behaviors, and membership in a community of others who share those attractions."

I suppose overestimating gayness is understandable given the large footprint gay people – like Jews – have on culture, media, and politics. Still, I was mildly surprised to discover that, in all probability, just 1.7 percent of Americans between eighteen and forty-four identify as gay, though some surveys put the figure as high as 3.5 percent. The UK estimate is an equally modest 1.5 percent. A recent survey of the metropolitan New York City Jewish community found that fifty thousand individuals, or roughly 3.2 percent, were living in homosexual households. Similarly, in Chicago the statistic is that 3 percent of the community are gay.[2]

There are no airtight statistics for the percentage of Israel's population that is gay, though some gay activists absurdly claim 15 percent of Israelis are gay. It's probably reasonable to assume that the Israeli numbers are not dramatically different from those in the US or Britain.

What matters, of course, are less the statistics then the individuals behind them.

Rafi Bartov is a gregarious professor of comparative literature at a major Israeli university. Though resolutely secular from birth – "I couldn't

---

1. See for instance, Benoit Denizet-Lewis, "The Scientific Quest to Prove Bisexuality Exists," *The New York Times Magazine*, March 20, 2014.
2. I can't explain the discrepancy. It seems unlikely that a higher proportion of Jews are gay than the general population. If the numbers are skewed, the question is why? Parenthetically, demographers say that childlessness among non-Orthodox Jews – meaning the majority of Jewish people – irrespective of sexual orientation, is their greatest concern.

care less who will say Kaddish for me" – his Jewishness is reflected in how he thinks about himself, in how he identifies with others, in his Israeli nationality, and through his involvement with the Hebrew language. Ritual and synagogue play no part in his life, but, like other secular Israelis, he marks the seasonal holidays and, occasionally, Sabbaths with food and family gatherings. Rafi served me Rooibos tea in his cozy, book-lined home-office decorated with African artifacts collected during an overseas sabbatical.

I was curious about how Rafi related to his childlessness, and whether his attitude was substantively different from those of the other – presumably straight – men I'd spoken to. Like several of them – and like me – Rafi did not have a nurturing relationship with his father. With the kind of hindsight provided by years of psycho-analysis, Rafi painfully acknowledges that his father wanted to have a good relationship with him, but that from a remarkably early age, Rafi pushed him away. "I must have been afraid of his realizing that I was gay. You might say I, unconsciously, preemptively, created a distance between us. Unfortunately, my father died even before I came out to myself, let alone to him."

Rafi hopes that, one day, "a good gay psychologist" will write a book about the straight-father gay-son dynamic. He believes its consequences play out at an extremely early stage of personality development. "If one goes down the Freudian path, one can envisage variations of the Oedipus construct, which typically involves the parent of the opposite sex, applied to a straight father and gay son. Is the son unknowingly tempting the father sexually? Does the father have to reject his own unconscious attraction to the son?"

In heterosexual children, this phase ends when the child identifies with the parent of the same sex. So Rafi wonders if the "effeminate son" may – in a twist on the Freudian model – be trying to tempt the father sexually.

As a fifty-something gay man, Rafi says emphatically that he relates to his childlessness differently from straight men his age, "because to some degree, I'd never expected to have children. Knowing that I am gay, I just assumed – it depended on my age and the period in my life – that I'd be both miserable and childless."

Indeed, the prospect of not becoming a father was the least of his worries. In high school, Rafi was preoccupied with trying to convince himself that he was not gay, even though he knew he was. That continued to be his preoccupation for many years.

After his army service, Rafi spent an extended period of time in London. "By the time my straight friends started getting married and having children, I was out of Israel. I was relieved to be in London, not so much because of the children issue as because of the marriage business – not having to attend weddings and weddings, and more weddings.

"When I did find myself at one, I felt out of place. I didn't have a partner at the time. I was not completely out of the closet. So being the odd man out at yet another wedding was something I couldn't tolerate, and I was very happy to be out of the country as much as possible. Having a broken heart because all the people around me were starting to have children didn't really figure large – not at that stage." First, there had to be love.

Only after Rafi was in a long-term relationship with his current partner, Geoffrey – a fellow academic he met at a seminar – did he "suddenly realize that my 'biological clock' was ticking. I decided that I needed to have children. And in this need, I connected to the Jewish or Israeli obsession with children." Rafi makes this observation about the gay couples he and Geoffrey know in the UK and US: "Those who are raising children and for whom it is important to have a child are almost all Israelis or Jewish."

When Rafi was already 40, he and Geoffrey, who is a few years older, agreed that they should have a child. But Rafi was the one driven by the idea. "For me it was beyond any rational thought process. I'm convinced it was tied to my Judaism. Geoffrey, who's more Jewishly literate than many US Jews [though he is not Jewish himself], believes it was Holocaust-related. For him, it is self-evident: So many Jews had been killed that I had to compensate. I had to create new Jews."

Having children translated into surrogacy. Both men were teaching at universities in California at the time, making the process expensive but otherwise undemanding. They located the right agency, which specialized in finding surrogate mothers and, separately, egg donors, and were in a very advanced stage of the process. The plan was that Rafi would become a stay-at-home dad.

Then Geoffrey was offered a career-making job offer that required them to move out of state. Suddenly, surrogacy became logistically and legally difficult, not to mention financially prohibitive, given the need to fly back and forth regularly to California.

Then, just as Rafi was trying to reconcile himself to remaining childless, his sister, who at the time was single and living in Tel Aviv, announced that she was carrying twins after undergoing IVF. Rafi's paternal instincts had found a much-needed outlet.

As much as his own path has been rocky, it is clear to Rafi that the younger generation of gay men is not hesitant when it comes to children. "It's plain to my younger Israeli gay friends that having children is connected to their Israeli and Jewish identity. I have many gay friends, couples, younger than us, they don't even ask themselves why or how. It is patently obvious to them that being gay Israelis – being Jewish – does not mean that they are not going to have children. In fact, they are as obsessed with having children as straight Israeli couples. I can think of couples who are relatively poor – still graduate students – yet are putting all their money into surrogacy. It is apparent that this is what gay male couples do."

In the United States, where progressive streams of Judaism sometimes conflate Judaism and liberalism, American Jews are front and center in their overwhelming backing for gay rights. But in Israel, issues like "gay marriage" are largely beside the point. First, there is no separation between "church and state" in Israel; and second, the country's established "church" – which oversees matters that in New York City, for instance, would often fall under the purview of the Family Court – is Orthodox Judaism.

Orthodox Judaism limits the rights of the individual – both straight and gay – vis-à-vis the state. One consequence is that Israeli gay men do not have the option of domestic surrogacy, IVF, or local adoption. On the positive side, national laws already provide gay couples with legally sanctioned partnerships. Thus, what matters most to Israel's pragmatically minded gay couples is creating a family. One primary channel for surrogacy was recently closed when Indian authorities barred overseas gays from employing Indian surrogate mothers. Meanwhile, other doors are opening as Israeli courts and medical ethicists continue to hash out parameters that could facilitate domestic surrogacy for gays (and others).

These days, Rafi divides his time between life with Geoffrey, who is based in New England, and his own university teaching in Israel. Down the line, when circumstances allow, the couple plan to set up home permanently in Israel so they can be closer to their nephews. Rafi continues to derive a great deal of happiness from helping to raise his sister's twins, who are now elementary-school age. "There is something more here about *family* than about me, the individual," he says. "Both Geoffrey and I invest a huge amount of time and love in my nephews."

Still, he says, it is sharing his deep love of literature with his students that gives him the greatest satisfaction. "Teaching gives my life meaning," he tells me. "It is in the same emotional place where fatherhood sits. I have raised – I am raising – generations of children." Teaching, for Rafi, is clearly a form of paternity. "I have always been aware that I cannot maintain a standoffish academic relationship with my students, though it goes without saying that I don't cross any lines.

"Yet I do have relationships that have become very personal. Most of my friends today were once my students – so that involvement has always been there. I get involved in their personal lives. Geoffrey and I invite them to dinner, and they invite us, and we occasionally travel together. My best friend in Jerusalem is a woman who is an ex-student. She's also a single mom, and I have taken a significant role in raising her children."

Rafi wonders if this father-mentor phenomenon is an attribute particularly pronounced among gay men. It occurs to him that his good friend, a renowned gay classicist based in New York, happens to be one of the most committed teachers and mentors he's ever encountered – and the biological father to several children of a straight friend. For Rafi, this connection between mentoring and fatherhood is palpable. "This is who I am."

Having been generously open about his own way of coping with biological childlessness, Rafi provides me with a rare insight into one intersection between the gay and *haredi* worlds that contains not a little pathos.[3] He tells me the following story. An ex-student – ultra-Orthodox, though not insular in the *haredi* manner (or else he would not have been attending university in the first place) – emailed him out of the blue urgently seeking an appointment. "'You are the only gay man I know. Will you help find a religious Israeli gay man willing to have a child with my sister?'"

The student's sister, it transpired, did not want a traditional marriage, but did want a baby. After lots of furtive back-and-forth, the student revealed what Rafi suspected all along: that the sister was gay and needed a marriage of convenience. They might get married and have children – perhaps through IVF – but there would be no sexual demands on either side. Outwardly, they would be a couple. Privately, they'd keep each other's sexual orientation a closely guarded secret. In her blinkered world, coming out as a lesbian was not an option. But neither was lifelong singlehood and childlessness.

Rafi consented to make some inquiries, putting the student in touch with a few contacts. The episode drove home an appreciation that even in the ultra-Orthodox community, there is an awareness of "work-arounds" that can make it possible for lesbians and gay men to straddle two opposing worlds.

In the modern Orthodox world, too, increasing numbers of women who either can't find suitable marriage partners or are simply not interested in having a sexual relationship with a man are having children

---

3. Strides have been made by observant gays to call attention to their concerns. The 2001 film, *Trembling Before G-d*, by director Sandi Simcha Dubowski, is a US-made documentary about the struggles of Orthodox gays and lesbians to reconcile faith and sexuality. Orthodykes runs a website for Orthodox Jewish lesbians. *Keep Not Silent*, a documentary film about Jewish lesbians, was released in 2004.

on their own.[4] Among his modern Orthodox female students, and despite the fact that the halachic obligation of procreation is on the man and not the woman, "it's become immensely important to have children – maybe even more important than marriage itself."

The more time he's spent abroad, extended by having a partner not from Israel, the more he's become mindful that in Judaism, having children is the paradigm for life. "I think Israel is the only country where upper-middle-class couples have more than one child, where the standard is three. We are a children factory. It has become taken for granted."

So what will you leave behind? I press. "My books will be read for maybe ten years and then someone else will write a better book, but my students – fine, they will not live forever and many will forget me – but it will take fifty years, and not ten."

---

4. The angst associated with being modern Orthodox ("national religious" in Israeli parlance) of marriageable age – yet frustratingly, exasperatingly, seemingly indefinitely single – was exquisitely portrayed in the Hebrew-language television series *Srugim*, broadcast on Israel's YES network between 2008–2012. Even the haunting theme song *Ana Efne* ("Where Do I Turn To?") captures the pathos of what it means to be without a romantic partner – and thus intimacy and the prospect of children. Orthodox 20- and 30-somethings live in a milieu which does not sanction premarital sex, demands strict religious observance, yet exposes them to the temptations of the larger world of which they are a part.

Chapter 20

The Small Matter of the Meaning of Life

When I decided to write a book about coming to grips with childlessness, one of the first people I told was Saul Singer, who had been a colleague and mentor of mine at *The Jerusalem Post* and later wrote the bestseller *Start-Up Nation*. The first words out of his mouth were, "I'd always assumed you and Lisa just made a decision not to have kids." Followed by, "The dilemma of childlessness forces a person – and not just a Jewish person – to consider the very meaning of life."

Saul is among the most cerebral people I know. And as he sipped his latte, I realized that he had just helped me crystallize the line of inquiry I wanted to pursue for this book – exploring the meaning of life without children.

As to Saul's impression that Lisa and I didn't want kids, I realized that on a subconscious level, I had probably wanted people to think precisely that. Better to be perceived as selfish than as hapless.

For Saul, and for many other committed Jews, and as affirmed by several of the childless men I spoke to, the purpose of life is *tikkun olam*, a mystical concept best defined as mending or restoring our broken world. In practical terms, it's doing good. Doing right. Pursuing the best course of life. As Saul sees it, children are the standard, preferred way to give life meaning, a conduit, if you will, for *tikkun olam*. Offspring not as an end in themselves, but a means.

So on a bright, mild winter's day, I sat in a suburban park not far from Jerusalem with Dan Lobel to hash out Saul's idea about *tikkun olam*. You'll recall Dan – he and his wife Tzipi started IVF, and when that didn't work initiated the process of adoption, only to be sidetracked when Dan discovered he had cancer.

"I would say that *tikkun olam* is definitely a central goal," Dan observes, "but that it has to be done, or chiefly done, through children? I can see why people who have children would think that, because it's really where all their energy and focus go for the best years of their lives. But I don't think it's necessarily so."

So what *is* the purpose of life if you don't leave anything behind biologically? "First of all," Dan replies, "I don't think leaving stuff behind biologically is the only way to leave a lasting legacy. Whether it is in writing a book with shelf-life, or helping out in a soup kitchen…" Dan breaks for a sip of water. He can't speak for long periods as a result of the after-effects of radiation treatments.

"I would say everything we do can – and should – be *tikkun olam*. Absolutely everything. Making a benediction when you eat something and recognizing this food came to you from God. Or when you're filling your car with petrol and helping someone struggling to unscrew their gas cap; everything is *tikkun olam*."

Dan's view of *tikkun olam* is much more than acting toward others with kindness. It's all-encompassing – from the personal to the global. It is also "about building yourself up; working through your own issues; trying to realize your own spiritual potential on a personal level. And if it's not going to be through children, that doesn't mean you can't do it, or shouldn't do it."

I think this was Saul's point too.

Dan's emphasis is, however, different, more explicitly God-centered. He tells me that Judaism places no higher value on the Ten Commandments – the Cecil B. DeMille shock-and-awe setting in which they were handed down at Mount Sinai notwithstanding – than on the comparatively banal civil jurisprudence regulations found liberally sprinkled elsewhere throughout the Hebrew Bible. Dan's point is that "there is *no* non-religious act, ultimately. Everything we do can enhance God's presence in the world. So I think there are a lot of 'offspring' that are not necessarily biological."

Fine, I say, but why does Judaism so stigmatize the childless? Am I the only one who bristles at the prejudice against childless men as a collective? Dan acknowledges that until I began *hocking* him on the subject he hadn't given it much thought, and that it does add up to a certain *Weltanschauung*. Yet he has never personally felt devalued as a Jew because he is not a father. Not even remotely. For me, that's not precisely the point. I also never felt individually stigmatized for not being a father. But I am cognizant of being part of a collective that culture, community, and tradition have set apart. Maybe my sensitivity is sharpened by the Pater's harping, his boundless faith as against my perplexity.

Where I have issues with my Father Above and my earthly father, Dan has solid, healthily evolving relationships with both. He could never be angry with either. He believes God does indeed micromanage our lives, and, regardless of how things pan out, knows what He's doing. Pacing himself to stave off exhaustion, Dan explains: "I look at my physical size versus the solar system, the universe, and realize that I am really small. I don't have any problem with the concept, therefore, that in addition to my physical smallness, I am also intellectually small. It's a metaphor for my position in the universe. And that I don't understand everything that's going on doesn't bother me; I would *like* to understand everything – maybe that would be enlightening. But there are things that are beyond me. I can't even direct my stomach to digest my food. In the same way, there are things beyond my ken intellectually, too."

I genuinely envy Dan's religious conviction, one that claims that because clear-cut answers are not within our human grasp, the match necessarily falls to God. I just don't have it in me to let the Creator so easily off the hook. I find it difficult to believe that God is at once micromanaging our mundane lives – in the sense that He intervenes *personally* in them – and that these interventions are, presumably, for the best; yet also forever beyond human understanding. It may sound hackneyed, but I can't help asking: Was it really for the best that the Pater's father and sister were killed by the Nazis? Or, for that matter, that Lisa and I have been denied children?

I'm completely with Dan about there being plenty not to understand. For myself, I try to keep in mind Donald Rumsfeld's "unknown unknowns" hypothesis and Nassim Taleb's Black Swan theorem. To wit: We never have a complete understanding of what's currently happening, much less the capability of anticipating game-changing events still on the horizon. But this brings me to a different place.

For no matter how you spin it, contemporary sensibilities make it hard to justify Judaism's denigration of the childless. Granted, no single source, text, folklore tidbit, or sound bite serves to encapsulate what "Judaism says" on the subject, but the sum total of what we have is pretty damning.

In my quest to give God a right of rebuttal in this book, I was interested to read a piece not long ago in the journal *Sh'ma* by Aryeh Cohen, associate professor of rabbinic literature at California's Ziegler School of Rabbinic Studies, which tackled the issue of "troubling texts."[1] Namely, what are we to do with canonized or divinely inspired texts that upset our moral sensibilities, "that jar our moral equilibrium"?

---

1. See "Dealing with Troubling Texts," http://www.myjewishlearning.com/texts/About_Jewish_Texts/Jewish_Texts/Troubling_Texts.shtml.

"Would a holy mouth say something like this? Would a holy text say something like this?" Cohen asks. These are the very questions that spring to mind when I read the opprobrium in which sages and Jewish folklorists hold the childless. Cohen offers a tripartite road map for dealing with such jarring material: Silence. Questioning. Dissent.

> When Moses tells Aaron that Aaron's sons have been killed, Aaron's response is silence. The silence, it seems, is his acknowledgement that this, too, is "a way of God." It might be a way of God that is problematic, [but] it is still a way of God. Aaron's silence lets the impact of the death and tragedy hang in the air.

Aaron's silent approach allows a sacred text to "wash over" the reader "without the vitiation of apologetics."

> The second step is modeled after Abraham's interaction with God concerning the destruction of Sodom and Gomorrah. When God tells Abraham that God is about to destroy the cities, Abraham addresses God: "Shall not the Judge of all the earth do justly?" That is, is God in this situation living up to the ethical standard that God demands?

Cohen notes that Abraham's questioning does not make any special allowances for the arguably barbaric milieu in which God's decision is being made.

> The third step is modeled after Moses' argument with God following the incident of the Golden Calf. When God seeks to destroy the People of Israel, Moses dissents: "Forgive your people – or if not, blot me, I pray Thee, out of Thy book which Thou hast written" (Exodus 32:32).

Silence. Questioning. Dissent.

Still, this three-pronged approach doesn't satiate my needs when faced with the canon on childlessness. All I can do is accept that answers are elusive and relish the seeking process; for me, the spiritual journey will always trump uncritical faith. I need to see philosophers and theologians at least *try* to provide the Creator with alibis to explain everything – from the destruction of European Jewry and the most recent natural disaster to the daily sufferings of the righteous; in other words, "why bad things happen to good people."

If you don't grapple with theodicy – reconciling evil in a world where God is omnipotent – can you even have a relationship with God? The answer for many believers is yes. In her recent book *When God Talks Back: Understanding the American Evangelical Relationship with God*, Stanford anthropologist T.M. Luhrmann argues that for evangelical Christians, God is not an explanation but a relationship resembling that of a client and therapist. I imagine that my father and other ultra-Orthodox Jewish believers see God in a similar vein. While the approach does not work for me, I'm as uncomfortable with putting the Creator of the Universe in the dock as with letting Him entirely off the hook.

There are times when I'm content with the disappearance-of-God theory popularized best by Prof. Richard Elliott Friedman of the University of California. According to Friedman, for God's own reasons He has disappeared from our lives just as He incrementally vanishes in the narrative from Genesis to Chronicles. God is on every page of Genesis, Exodus, and so on; but an attentive Bible reader will see Him ever so slowly disappear – so that by the end of the canon He's practically vanished. I think Friedman's point is that maybe He wants us to be as independent, rationalist, skeptical, and pragmatic as we can be.

Maybe God's intentions are not static. Maybe, following Maimonides, all we can really say about God is what He is not. It is easy to concede that God could have some – unknowable to me – cosmic reason why I should remain childless. Still, let me turn the question the other way: If the fertile are thus blessed, why are so many parents unfit to raise the children God has gifted them with? Literally down the street from where I live, on a wonderful, balmy Jerusalem morning, a mother stabbed her two small children to death, then tried to kill herself. A few days later, as if an epidemic of depravity had been unleashed, a father kidnapped his two small children from the Tel Aviv home of his estranged wife, threw them off the roof of a nearby building, then jumped to his own death. In both of these cases, the blessings of fertility were undeniably, horrifically profaned. Not to mention that the history of humanity is, overwhelmingly, about countless generations of unremarkable parents begetting a planet full of run-of-the-mill children. The quantity of offspring makes Darwinian sense, but to uncritically call them all blessings seems a bit of a stretch.

This notion was brought home to me when I recently read J.K. Rowling's rather maligned *The Casual Vacancy*, a book that unsparingly illustrates the continuum of ordinary parents begetting ordinary children who aren't necessarily an unmitigated blessing. One could make the case that Rowling is suggesting that parenthood isn't for everyone; that lost souls sometimes want children for the wrong reasons; that there are parents who deserve better children than biology delivers; and that adoption doesn't necessarily paper over deep psychic hurts. At the end of the day, maybe there are neither blessed nor cursed. Or maybe we need to rethink what we mean by those words in matters of procreation.

Chapter 21

A Thousand Years of Faith

Yehezkel Gabbay speaks in the manner I imagine a philosopher longshoreman from Brooklyn might. Someone who, were he not wearing a deliberately nondescript *kipa*, could be played by Robert De Niro. He was already waiting for me at the kosher Tel Aviv café on Arlosoroff Street where we'd arranged to meet. "Call me Hezie," he says.

Unique among the childless men who shared their stories with me, Hezie already knew by age 24 that he and his wife Ronit, who was 22 at the time, were unlikely to ever be parents.

Hezie is Sephardi and, as we speak, it quickly becomes clear that his Iraqi heritage informs every fiber of his body, his worldview, and his attitude about childlessness. He professes to be a man of certainties; to know the best course of life. He knows where he comes from, and what God expects of him.

He married at 24. Within six months he realized children were "gonna be a long shot." He didn't agonize over adoption, because, as he puts it, "I didn't feel any desire to raise a kid that's not mine." In retrospect, he grants that his wife would have liked to discuss the matter further. But he's in no doubt about the decision they would have come to. "It is rare to meet an adopted kid that doesn't have issues," he says. And in his tight-knit Iraqi community, everyone would have known the child was adopted, making it even more challenging for the boy or girl.

Hezie took his cue, he tells me, from "an old Kew Gardens guy," a childless widower now in his 90s, whom he describes as "a giant all around" – meaning in his mastery of Torah and success as an entrepreneur. They had a one-off discussion on the matter when Hezie first found out his situation. The older man, a sort of mentor, told him that after tests showed that he and his wife were not going to ever be parents, the doctor asked him if he loved his wife. He said he did. "OK, then. Go out and have a good life. You ain't having kids."

"We all want a lot of things in life. But there are curve balls, and I would not trade this issue for any other. Why? Because it is ours! And we must find the faith and strength to deal with it…. We cannot allow ourselves to obsess with this one mitzva, however great, to the point where our lives are turned upside down."

Although Hezie doesn't tell me outright, I know that he is a *Ḥakham*, the Sephardi equivalent of a rabbi. His background is evident in the references he drops into the conversation, even if it's tricky to reconcile his scholarship with the cadence of his speech. Though he devotes much energy and resources to *tikkun olam*, he bristles when I make mention of it. He doesn't like anything that smacks of political correctness. "We Sephardim do it anyway as a way of life," he says.

There's no beginning to understand how Hezie has come to terms with being a childless man without understanding his rock solid faith and deep roots in his community. He likes to keep things simple and neatly pigeonholed.

He sometimes thinks that Ashkenazim and Sephardim are from different planets. Which is why the more he learns about my own story, the more he thinks I am coming at the whole childlessness issue wearing Ashkenazi blinkers: that I'm over-thinking it. Placing too much weight on folktales and commentators he doesn't put much stock in.

Hezie and his Ronit both come from the same homogenous Iraqi Jewish Queens, NY neighborhood. Their families knew one another like everyone knew everyone else. They saw each other in synagogue, had friends in common. With his father's permission, he took Ronit to a Mets baseball game on their first date. Before giving him the green light, however, his father made inquiries about the girl and her family, and her folks had a chance to assess his character when he came to pick her up. "There was none of that 'honk the horn and the girl comes out,'" he says. Pretty much from the second or third date, they knew they would be a couple. So long as their parents approved, of course. It all sounds pretty old world. But that's how he was raised.

When people began to realize that babies were not happening for the newly married couple – "we are a high-profile couple in the community" – they made the decision to speak openly about their fertility problems. "We were like, a poster couple of childlessness." They gave seminars on infertility to the community. He took communal and synagogue leadership positions. Sometimes he felt a bit awkward asking parents to control their children during services, but he did it anyway. It was harder on Ronit. Her relationship with God was more "complicated." For both of them there was hurt, pain, and disappointment. But there was no anger at God – not then and not now.

He attributes their reaction to their sense of place. Both come from a long line of Iraqi rabbis, scholars, and communal leaders. "We're talking generations of faith. Rabbis on my father's side, and my mother's side, and on Ronit's father's side. A thousand years of faith.

"Either you believe what you believe or you don't believe. Either you are who you are or you're a fraud. You need to live your faith. So if you say every day, 'I believe,' then, comes one day when you face hardship, what do you say, 'well, really, I was joking?'"

He'd rather focus on what God has given them. "He's given us health. He's given us money. He's given us companionship. He gives us a big extended family. He gives us community. He gives us common sense. How are you angry at God who gives you life?"

Once a week, Hezie studies Torah with a scholar from a related, prominent Sephardi family. His study partner has been in a wheelchair since he was a child. "The guy is about my age. He's got no children. He's not married. He's in a wheelchair. How can I look at him and be angry when he's so happy to be studying Torah?"

When the holidays come around, he and Ronit make it a point to have large family gatherings at their place, with lots of children running around.

Interestingly, the thing about not having children that has been the hardest for Hezie was the loss of friends. He and Ronit found socializing with couples who had children to be an aching bore. "All these folks wanted to talk about was their kids," he says. And so, their social circle began to shrink.

"God bless you, but let me in on the conversation. I don't want to sit there like an idiot," Hezie recalls himself thinking. "You find that your old friends are making new friends through their kids' schools. You start losing friends."

Hezie and Ronit invest lots of love in their many nieces and nephews. They've also been foster parents in their home, and helped pay for the weddings of young people they took under their wings. "Call it, 'give a kid a break.'" He makes his living in finance, but his avocation is teaching at a local yeshiva and sharing his love for Torah study. It gives him immense satisfaction. And you can tell he is the kind of teacher whose enthusiasm is infectious.

Still, deep down, they have not given up on the possibility that God will yet reward them with a child. Over the years, Hezie has kept up with scientific advances in fertility treatments. Over the years, too, they've done cycles of IVF treatments. They decided not to allow infertility to become all-consuming, but when he hears about some experimental approach, he does his research.

"'Cause you never know. We have faith in the *Ribbono Shel Olam* – the Master of the World – and so we also have hope. Now, whether hope is a good thing or a bad thing…that's up for discussion.

Maimonides writes about God not interfering in what happens in nature. But that does not mean that God can't intervene if He wanted to. Which means that there is always hope. I never give up hope. Every month up till now. You know what? I like it that way. I also like a good cry every now and then."

Chapter 22

Yad Vashem

I'm still searching for a defense counsel, someone to offer perspective to my bill of particulars charging Judaism's canon with disrespect, disregard, even disdain for the childless. And I may have found the right man in one Joseph Isaac Lifshitz, an Orthodox pulpit rabbi and philosopher at Jerusalem's Shalem College.[1]

Over tea and biscuits in my kitchen, the courteous, soft-spoken Lifshitz thinks a good place to start is with the idea that Judaism does indeed attach a theological element to family. To underscore this "theology of couplehood," he reprises a well-known homily often told under the marriage canopy. It goes like this: The Hebrew word for man is *ish*, spelled *aleph-yud-shin*. For woman the word is *isha*, spelled *aleph-shin-hay*. The letters *yud* and *hay* combine to form the

---

1. Rav Lifshitz first came to my attention when I covered a Jerusalem conference on Jews and capitalism. Our paths occasionally crossed subsequently at social and academic gatherings. But this was the first time we sat down to discuss theology.

name for God. Removing the letters *yud* and *hay* – i.e., removing God! – from the words (man) *ish* and (woman) *isha* leaves the letters *aleph* and *shin*, spelling *esh* – the word for inferno.

Judaism teaches that if God does not dwell amongst newlyweds, what's left will be…a hellhole. The same idea relates to family. The Talmud says if a child respects his parents, then God is present; if not, He isn't. Afterward, I reflect that maybe God has not been present in my life because I did not respect my absent father. That seems a bit unsporting. Anyway, Rav Lifshitz has illuminated why there is something Godly about family.

Now comes the "on the other hand."

Consider the haftara recited on Jewish fast days other than Yom Kippur, which is taken from Isaiah 56:5: "Even unto them will I give in My house and within My walls a monument and a memorial – a *Yad Vashem* – better than sons and daughters; I will give them an ever-lasting memorial, that shall not be cut off."[2] It's a lesson about continuity, says Lifshitz; that at the End of Days, God is going to compensate those without family with something better than children.

Lifshitz continues: "So, on the one hand, you find a theological idea of children – it's the first mitzva or commandment. On the other hand, you have this prophecy that tells you there is a possibility of something greater." Perhaps the most profound message of covenantal Judaism, according to Lifshitz, is the notion of productivity. "If man can produce another human being, he is obligated to do so – but procreation is not the only production that a person can do."

With a nod to my current project, Lifshitz suggests that "writing a book can be something greater; or teaching, or enhancing spirituality and understanding of the religion. These are no less meritorious than having children."

Lifshitz, who comes from a distinguished rabbinical line, was born in Geneva to a Swiss mother and an Israeli father. His father,

---

2. Yad Vashem is also the name of Israel's official Holocaust memorial, museum, and research center based in Jerusalem. It is the only such institution that I'm aware of whose express purpose isn't to subtly universalize the Shoah and underplay Zionism.

Rabbi Haim Lifshitz, studied Torah with Rabbi Yechiel Yaakov Weinberg, a major twentieth-century *posek*, or decisor of Jewish law. He also studied psychology with the famed Jean Piaget. While the elder Lifshitz combined Torah and psychology, his son works to harmonize philosophy and Torah.

"Man has to produce as much as he can," Lifshitz explains. "And 'can' is different in every person. So I think the main value is to be like God – *imitatio Dei* – by producing, by creating. The simplest creation that man can do is having children. It's amazing, effortless for most. You don't have to be too intelligent to procreate. And it's not your fault if you don't. If a person is intellectual, or can give to others in some other fashion – this is another way."

Lifshitz believes that man should aim to be God-like. From his father, Lifshitz learned that the road to God is paved with creativity. Another sip of tea while I bombard Lifshitz with the litany of nasty, superstitious declarations made in the Torah, Talmud, Zohar, and folktales about the childless. "I don't know how seriously to take them," he responds. "You know what Maimonides says in *The Guide for the Perplexed*? I love this book. I've just finished teaching it for the third time. Maimonides talks about so-called punishments in the Bible. Everybody, famously, cites his dismissive views about animal sacrifices at the ancient Temple. He implies that animal sacrificing was God's way of dealing with ancient Israel in that primitive milieu. The Torah has a way of communicating with simple people: for simple people, if they don't get rewarded or punished, they don't get the message. Maimonides states that the Torah competes in a world where other religions promise all kinds of things. OK, so God also promised goodies.

"Of course not having children is a punishment – of a subjective nature. You can also take it as punishment that you are not wealthy, if all you want is materialism. Or you can take it as just a fact. The Hazon Ish, Rabbi Abraham Yishayahu Karelitz was childless, as was my father's famed Talmud partner, Rav Weinberg." In fact, Rabbi Weinberg left his wife early in their marriage, convinced that his scholarship would otherwise suffer. "Nothing will come out of you if you continue to devote yourself to your family," Rav Weinberg told Lifshitz's father. "Obviously, my father did not take that advice. But at some level, Rav Weinberg was right," says Lifshitz. "There is a price for having children, too."

Fine, I say, but none of this obviates institutionalized stigma – in ancient days, we childless men couldn't serve on the Sanhedrin, and nowadays we can't lead High Holy Day services.

Lifshitz doesn't buy it. "That stems from a need people feel to start from the personal. If the *ḥazan*, a prayer leader, has children, he has mercy on them, so he'll cry more. Some congregations like the display of emotionalism. But it's not such a value. So you don't go in front of the *amud* (lectern), so what? And, besides, it is only symbolic. Congregants without children are, in reality, invited to *daven* – there is no prohibition – it's a recommendation that people violate all the time.

"I won't take it seriously. With the Sanhedrin, it is exactly the same principle. You know the Ḥofetz Ḥaim was asked to pick a prayer leader…there was a good cantor, who was not such a big *tzaddik* – or a *tzaddik* who was not such a good cantor; so the great rabbi said, '*First* he should be a cantor.' In other words, first get someone who knows his job. Let me assure you, if the Ḥazon Ish had been willing to be a cantor, no one would have been bothered because the sage wasn't a father."

All true, I press, but if you consolidate all the off-putting invectives the canon has thrown at the childless – we're like the dead, fit only for reincarnation – rather than sprinkle them episodically here and there, the blows become devastating.

While Lifshitz agrees, he stresses that "Your obligations, as a Jew, are largely in the spiritual realm. Yes, we have mitzvot and halakha, but remember what the sages taught: 'It is not incumbent upon you to complete the work, but neither are you at liberty to desist from it' (Avot 2:21)."

Lifshitz's point is that just as you don't need to observe all of Torah, perfection is not expected in the sphere of procreation. Judaism is a practical creed, yet there is an element in which it is similar to Eastern religions. "Life is a journey. You work with what you have, and you use the qualities that you have, and the talents that you have to do your best," he says.

Wait. So why does Jewish folklore get entangled in promulgating superstitious nonsense about the childless? Don't most ultra-Orthodox Jews, and maybe Orthodox ones too, buy into the *kaddish'l* business? The Pater – together with his *haredi* and hasidic world – doesn't speak in metaphor. Which is, I grant, ironic considering that Orthodox Jews are the opposite of Bible literalists.

Am I testing his patience? It seems not. Lifshitz is a man of faith who is also a rationalist. And he's quick to acknowledge that having faith is not something one achieves intellectually. "Just as some people are tone deaf to music, others are religiously deaf to God."

He resumes. "Look, I am a cousin of Rav Joseph Ber Soloveit-chik. What you're describing…," he pauses as if to prepare me for his next words, "our family, we have a different religion.[3] Let me give you an example. My father passed away on Sukkot, five months ago, and when it came time to say Kaddish, which was after Simhat Torah, I didn't say Kaddish – and I am the rabbi of the shul. The next day, too, I didn't say Kaddish, so congregants asked me why. I said, 'Well, there was another mourner in shul, someone else saying Kaddish, so I didn't recite *my* Kaddish over *his* Kaddish – I didn't want a cacophony.' So they asked, when will you say Kaddish? I replied, 'When you permit me one singular Kaddish a day when no one else is saying it – then I will recite Kaddish.' You know how it is when a bunch of mourners all stand up at once and say Kaddish. A complete lack of decorum.

"Today I *davened* the morning prayers at the house of a neighbor who is sitting *shiva*, and again I didn't say Kaddish. People looked at me like, what are you religious for? My answer is: I have a different

---

3. Rabbi Soloveitchik (1903–1993), the great Orthodox philosopher and talmudist, was notable, too, for breaking with his ultra-Orthodox contemporaries in supporting the Zionist enterprise. He became honorary chairman of Mizrachi, the Orthodox Zionist faction in America. More generally, he also rejected *haredi* insularity, instead championing secular higher education.

religion. There is an idea behind why you are saying Kaddish – namely, that my father educated me well, and my father is happier that I am a gentle person, not fighting over saying the loudest Kaddish, and not disturbing someone else.

"Maybe some would find my elitism appalling, but the mob have their religion, and we follow a different, I would say, *refined* Judaism. The superstitious claptrap of the masses doesn't impress me at all," Lifshitz declares firmly, though without raising his voice.[4] "So what does matter?"

Like others I spoke with, Lifshitz believes the purpose of life is *tikkun olam*, mending the world. "The idea of *tikkun olam* comes from the Gemara. You know, there is a talmudic discussion. The background is that a slave is permitted to marry a slave; a free man is permitted to marry a free woman.

"Let's say there is a person who is a half-slave. How is he half? He had two owners, one of whom freed his part. So there is a portion of this servant that is free, and a portion that is a slave – consequently, he can't marry anyone. Therefore the Gemara says the other owner must also free the slave because otherwise the slave can't marry, and that would make him unproductive. The point? The sages want to underscore a larger lesson: God created the world so that we could be productive. Plainly, the most primitive, physical way of being productive is procreation. But there are other ways," he insists.

Lifshitz sees no shortage of empathy in Judaism. The sages don't approve of Jacob's technically correct, though callous response to Rachel's "Give me children – or else I die," when he replies, "Am I in God's stead, who has withheld from you the fruit of the womb?" In Lifshitz's view, God punishes Jacob for his lack of compassion,

---

4. The iconoclastic idea that there can be one Jewish message for the masses and another for the elites is not everyone's cup of tea. My friend, Rabbi Jonathan Fishburn of London, a talmudist, an Orthodox progressive, and antiquarian book dealer, citing one of his teachers, Rabbi Nahum Eliezer Rabinovitch of Ma'aleh Adumim, tells me in his usual understated style that he finds the approach "a bit too neat."

for showing no mercy for Rachel's pain and tears. "She's crying. She wants children. We know that most people want to have children, and all the sources that you quoted, Elliot, relate to this wish. At the same time, the rabbis are saying that there are better ways to create."

Wait, I say, don't you mean *different* ways to create? "No. When I think about valuable ways, I really do mean better, because procreation is so basic. It is amazing, but there are ways to do *tikkun olam* that affect the world far more dramatically."

Lifshitz has been watching the film *A Late Quartet* on DVD. He thinks it contains a lesson worth sharing. There's a scene in which a famous concert violist has a fight with her daughter, who lashes out at her for putting career above family. She says something like, "I grew up without a mother at home."

That got Lifshitz worrying that maybe his children sometimes feel that way about him. He has friends who spend much more time with their children than he does. Instead of the concert hall, Lifshitz invests countless hours preparing his philosophy lectures and Torah lessons. There are students and congregants who depend on him. His children are paying the price of this dedication; he knows he could be a much bigger presence in their lives.

Yet he seems to have no regrets. "If all that you do is be a good father, in such a way that the wider world doesn't benefit from your other qualities, something is lacking. It's true that being a father is very important. On Shabbat, I teach from mid-afternoon until evening services. I am not in the house; for my family, it is not easy that I am the rabbi of a shul. They are used to it, but it's very difficult. It's not that I ignore them, yet I feel guilty that maybe I do not do enough. There is a price for *tikkun olam*."[5]

Lifshitz recalls a paper he once wrote about Jewish charity in the Middle Ages. It seems the Jewish community levied a tax, though

---

5. I shared Lifshitz's ideas with my friend George Mandel, who defended the opposite view: "Children only exist (and therefore have needs) because their parents created them. The parents therefore have a particular responsibility to their children which override any responsibility to the rest of the world."

it allowed for a deduction if one gave to relatives. At some point, the rabbis in medieval Ashkenaz, encompassing Germany and its environs, became uncomfortable with this deduction, which encouraged people to help their kin at the expense of others with possibly greater needs. The rabbis preferred that tithes go to the community at large. And to this end, they cited a talmudic passage which held that someone living in the time of the Temple who channeled his largesse, in the form of agriculture, to a single priest was like someone contributing to famine in the world.

"People focus so much on family. Family, family, family. It's become something of a mantra. For some, the family has become the religion. They don't have God, they have only family."

In the course of grappling with my childlessness, I have at the same time tried to understand why I jettisoned – first inwardly, then, much later, openly – my Orthodoxy. At the gut level, it was a sort of reprimand to God. On a deeper level, it was a reproof to Man who made up Orthodoxy, and to my father in particular, who embodied it in my childish imagination.

Lifshitz's theology is authentically Orthodox, yet it is appealingly progressive to me. When the Torah says something that appears to be immoderate, Lifshitz's reaction is toward contextualization. What is "orthodox" about his approach, Lifshitz says, is the simple fact that it goes along with all the sources – "I think it is, in fact, much more in harmony with Jewish tradition."

I tell Lifshitz that in my conversations with childless men, it strikes me that many lack the ability to trust in God – including those who would want to – because they feel let down by Him. I felt doubly let down by my Father in Heaven and my earthly father. So faith doesn't come easy. Yet rationalism is spiritually – meaning emotionally and psychologically – unsatisfying.

Lifshitz says that for him, blind ritual and rote behavior fail to meet Jewish standards. "I grew up thinking that you do have to look at the facts, you have to examine the seams, and you have to face the questions. That is the Judaism that I grew up on. I am sure that it is not good for everyone. It is not the way for the many. But it was the way of Rav Joseph Ber Soloveitchik. He demanded from himself and his students not only ritual, but a grounding in theology."

All religious "isms" come at two levels: ritual and practice is one; theology is the second. As Lifshitz implies, maybe there needs to be a version of Judaism that appeals to the baser, coarser, primordial needs of the masses. So that Orthodox Joe Six-Pack has a strict framework for living – the nuances implied by Maimonides' rationalism being beyond his ken. It's a rationalist elitist approach that appeals to me.

Chapter 23

Is Closure Possible?

Now that the aged Pater and I are reconciled, after a fashion, I find myself indulging him. For years, in conversations with Lisa, I found it emotionally difficult to talk about him as "my father." Nowadays, calling him "the Pater" has become part lark, though also habit. When I address him directly, however, I've switched from calling him "you" to "*Tateh*" (father).

I take without complaint his proffered pamphlets hawking holy men who promise to put an end to my childlessness. I shrug off automated telephone solicitations from miracle-making "charities," nearly certain that it was the Pater who gave them my number. Obviously, I don't tell him that I am no longer Orthodox. Why hurt him? Like I said, it's not as if the two of us have ever held a theological discussion. He realizes I do not spend my days studying the Talmud. He sees I do not wear the garb of the ultra-Orthodox.

He knows vaguely that I write for a living, though the details are of no interest. What matters, he takes pains to reiterate, is that

I use the impermanent presence of my time in this world to prepare for the World to Come – and that I sire a son who can say Kaddish after I'm gone.

Does he live with the fear that through my childlessness he is being punished for abandoning his only son? That God is punishing the son for the sins of the father? I can only speculate. The Pater will always remain an enigma.

If he has any capacity for introspection, it leads him not to greater self-awareness but ever deeper into the opiate of his dogma. Until he hit ninety, it was up at 4 a.m. for the *mikve* (ritual bath), then to sunrise prayers, followed by study, and then home to don a supplementary set of Rabbeinu Tam tefillin – for safety's sake – then back to the study hall and more prayers. This routine gave him comfort. He still gives money from his paltry income to the deserving and the charlatan alike. In his *ḥaredi* subculture, this is simply the norm. To me, his life is led in a haze of ritual and superstition; the altars of irrationality need constant stoking lest reality bite. Yet who am I to deny that his is an efficacious approach to forestalling the pain that comes with confronting one's innermost soul?

This I see clearly: To reach the comparatively good place he is in now, he had to jettison the American dream, his American wife, and – *you can't make an omelet without breaking a few eggs* – his American son.

I don't know how many visits and Friday phone calls my father and I have left. He's too infirm to come to Jerusalem. I've taken to visiting him and Devora weekly in Benei Berak, though he doesn't encourage it outright. He's superstitious about all the bad things that could befall me on the road. He's now confined to his apartment, unable to make it up and down the stairs. So my visits are more and more appreciated. His devoted younger daughter, Esti, tells me that my visits raise his spirits.

It pains me to find him unkempt, frail, and wobbly. His hearing is mostly gone. His eyes are failing. Still, he's as well looked after as possible, thanks to Esti, her husband Shai, and the magnificent local hasidic support network. Some years ago Esti, and Yossi, Devora's son from her second marriage, moved my father and his wife into a decent apartment. As he became increasingly unsteady, she arranged for a caregiver to take him to the *mikve*. Now, as his world becomes ever more constrained, a trip to the *mikve* is beyond reach.

Materially, his life has never been better – anyway, not since he left Avenue D. But he remains focused on "the future." He's asked me point-blank to say Kaddish for him when the time comes, and I've assured him that I'll be his *kaddish'l*. In an odd way, I've never felt closer to him, even if we remain, profoundly, strangers. He doesn't want me to be angry at him, and I've reassured him on that score.

I have lately taken to asking him for his blessing – the one fathers give their sons on the Sabbath. He puts his hands on my head: "May God make you like Ephraim and like Menashe. May the Lord bless you and protect you; may the Lord shine His countenance on you and be gracious to you; may the Lord favor you and grant you peace."

Before we part company he implores me to recite – thirteen times – the verse from Genesis 35:5, to which he attaches mystical protective value, prior to the drive back up to Jerusalem from Benei Berak. This I do. "*And they journeyed; and a terror of God was upon the cities that were round about them, and they did not pursue after the sons of Jacob.*" I now realize that the Pater has been looking out for me all along, from afar. He's employed every spiritual power in his arsenal.

I've taken to kissing his hands or even his bearded cheek good-bye when I take my leave. He walks haltingly to the stairwell to see me off, holding onto the walls for balance, letting me leave with the predictable, "*De zolts gibenchveren mit a ben zuchar*" – You should be blessed with a baby boy.

These days, I'm neither irritated by nor dismissive of his blessings. Not because I've all of a sudden become a believer in miracles. Rather, because I'm ever more certain that fatherhood would have suited me. With a son (or daughter) of my own, I might have demonstrated a capacity to be a good father in a different way than the Pater could achieve. But closure of that nature is not in the cards.

Closure, anyway, may be elusive and overrated. In a small gem of a book, *The Examined Life*, psychoanalyst Stephen Grosz writes that the counseling trade has put too much emphasis on closure. "My experience is that closure is an extraordinarily compelling fantasy of mourning. It is the fiction that we can love, lose, suffer and then do something to permanently end our sorrow. We want to believe we can reach closure because grief can surprise and disorder us – even years after our loss." He thinks that closure is ultimately "delusive," a "false hope that we can deaden our living grief."

"To Thine Own Self Be True"

Erev Rosh HaShana 5775

To steal a leaf from Leo Tolstoy's observation that "each unhappy family is unhappy in its own way" – I would say that every childless man has his own childlessness. For the most part, childless men don't feel comfortable talking about life without children. We endure childlessness as a background pain that we suppress, compartmentalize, and stifle. To save face and to spare the feelings of others, we tend not to bare our souls about what it means not to have children.

The truth is that although there is a void in my life, my life is not empty. Far from it. I consider myself a pretty fortunate fellow, blessed with a loving partner, a support network of good friends who are like family, and an extended family – some of whom are even friends.

This book is rooted in a lament but it also includes, I hope, heartening and wise ideas I picked up on my journey. This meditation gave me insights about my father, my mother, myself, and the creative process. It reinforced my intention not to give up on God. So at the end of the day, it's also a psalm of thanksgiving: "*You turned my lament into dancing, You undid my sackcloth and girded me with joy*" (Ps. 30:12–13).

I sought out other childless men to talk to, in part because I thought it would make this book less self-obsessed and lend context to my personal story. I learned a lot from the men I spoke with, but in the end, no one else's saga offered me emotional catharsis. Beyond our childlessness, there were not all that many common denominators. We all had differing relationships with our fathers and varying attitudes toward Judaism, though in my self-selected sample I didn't speak to anyone for whom Judaism was inconsequential. That said, I was the only one who'd latched on to the negative attitudes that tradition holds about the childless.

Nevertheless, there were important commonalities. None of us in relationships found them lacking for want of children. We all believe we'd have made good fathers. None of us feel our lives are not worth living because of our childlessness. As Lisa Manterfield, a California-based writer who runs a blog called "Life Without Baby," wrote recently, men probably prefer to grieve alone, albeit sometimes irritably. We're more likely to withdraw than to do "grief work"; we plan for the future rather than agonize about the present.[1]

I imagine some readers will feel that I overstated the extent to which Jewish tradition disparages the childless. After all, I never personally faced prejudice for being a childless man, nor did any of the men I interviewed. There is, it strikes me, a welcome disconnect between how sensitively (for the most part) ordinary people behave and what the tradition has sought to inculcate. My experience, by and large, is

---

1. See "Childless Men on Father's Day," *Life Without Baby*, June 10, 2013, http://lifewithoutbaby.com/2013/06/10/childless-men-on-fathers-day/.

that while people may see childlessness as a misfortune, they do not see it as a cause for censure. The canon's withering attitudes toward the childless may be intended not for the individual but for the nation.

Saul Singer points out that the uncompromising (my word) way Judaism deals with childlessness is not dissimilar to the way it relates to other lifestyles it seeks to discourage. Forming a nuclear family and raising children might not otherwise come naturally in a hypothetical state of nature. Being judgmental is what religion is all about, and part of being judgmental is putting niceties aside and adhering to unpalatable-sounding propositions for the greater good. "Being judgmental is built in to any religion's operating system," says Saul. To our modern sensibilities, what religions teach can feel jarring. Our task is to bridge the gap between the profound messages religion offers and its occasional discordances to modern ears.

Saul cites as an example the phrase at the end of the Grace After Meals: "I have been young and now I am old, but never have I seen the righteous man forsaken, nor his children begging for bread." There were times, Saul told me, when he refused to include this phrase in his prayers because it is patently untrue. I know I have felt the same. Ultimately Saul concluded that rather than being descriptive, the phrase needed to be read as a messianic-like aspiration. So the idea is: When canon throws you a curve ball, find a way to make sense of it without either compromising your integrity or throwing out the baby with the bathwater.

My father's obsession with my childlessness began as an irritant, yet over time it provided fodder for spiritual, emotional, and intellectual exploration – of which this book is the fruit. At the same time, there's no point in minimizing the psychological hurt I suffered as a result of growing up a fatherless only child. The Pater's departure felt like a betrayal. It left me angry, untrusting, and confused about what to expect from others. A self-defeating fear of betrayal imprinted itself on my psyche and informed many of my relationships, including my relationship with God.

I described my decision not to wear a *kipa* full-time as impelled by my childlessness. It was, sort of. But there is a back-story. I was never endowed with Vitamin Faith. Naturally, I tried to "have faith" and embrace the lessons I was taught in yeshiva. I tried to pray with fervor. As an Orthodox Jew, I was obliged, among other things, to believe that "God rewards those who keep His commandments" and that "the entire Torah that we now have is that which was given to Moses."

When precisely I stopped being theologically Orthodox I can't say for sure. Probably in my teen years, when I was compelled to choose between the passions of the body and the prohibitions of my rabbis. Those rabbis were supposedly conduits to God's wishes. God, though, had instilled me with inexorable desires, only to prohibit their enjoyment. That was annoying. Nor did I stumble upon many positive Orthodox role models in my twelve years-plus of yeshiva.

So I found myself living the life of a Marrano in reverse. These were the secret Jews whose conversion to Catholicism in late-1400s Spain was an artful, pragmatic dodge in the face of the wicked Inquisition authorities. For my part, even if my lifestyle was outwardly Orthodox, I was surreptitiously no longer "theologically Orthodox."

Yet I couldn't "come out" openly. First, it would have pained and embarrassed my mother, and let her down, to see that she'd failed to raise me as a "faithful Jew." If she were seen as having botched the job of raising me, it could mean only one thing: that Anshel was right about the spiritual emptiness of life outside the Holy Land – never mind that most Israelis lead non-observant lifestyles.

It meant so much to my mother to see me don tefillin and recite the morning prayers. She herself found succor in faith – though I imagine she had her own moments of doubt. In her later years, just like her own mother, she'd pass the hours with a book of Psalms in her hands. In any case, Mother and I lived in a homogenous Orthodox community. I wore my *kipa*. She wore her *sheitel*. I didn't seek confrontation. The truth is I barely knew *how* to be a Jew outside the boundaries of Orthodoxy.

And then came a Godsend. On a visit to Israel in the early 1990s, when my mother's mobility had become increasingly limited and we couldn't schlep up the stairs of the nearest Orthodox synagogue, we easily made it to a Conservative synagogue across from our Jerusalem hotel. The rabbi, Avraham Feder, turned out to be a brilliant orator, a Zionist intellectual, and also a melodious cantor. Not only that: it transpired that he was also my JDL chief Gene Singer's brother-in-law. Moreover, Feder himself had deep Lower East Side roots.

It was at Congregation Moreshet Yisrael on Jerusalem's Agron Street that Yvette and I sat next to one another – family style – for the first time in a shul. The idea of being an observant Conservative Jew opened up for me. Still, while she was alive, and even though, at my initiative, we became overseas members of Moreshet Yisrael, the only houses of worship I attended regularly were our Lower East Side neighborhood Orthodox congregations. I didn't discuss theology with my mother. Culturally, viscerally, primordially she was Orthodox.

My spiritual journey continues. My faith fluctuates, like a Wi-Fi signal. But my commitment to Jewish civilization and all it entails is unwavering. My Jewishness is imprinted on me, part of my operating system. In practice, I am Jewishly observant but make no claims to Orthodoxy. Lisa and I belong to both Conservative and Orthodox synagogues. I no longer hold God liable for every mishap in my life, yet paradoxically I am instinctively grateful to Him when things go smoothly.

So the childlessness issue was not the only catalyst for abandoning Orthodoxy. I stayed outwardly Orthodox for Yvette – when I visit the Pater I wear my *kipa* – but theologically and in terms of lifestyle, Orthodoxy is in my past. In all likelihood, had Lisa and I had children, chances are we'd be more scrupulous – read, more Orthodox – in our level of Jewish observance in order to "set an example." Our present approach embraces what we see as a Golden Mean, but I'm told that children need more clear-cut messages while they're growing up. That if there is even a whiff of two-facedness, youngsters are bound to sniff it out. Some of our friends seem to have found the right blend of religion and reason, so I suppose we'd have risen to the occasion, had we been put to the test.

Dan Lobel told me that seeing *yisurim,* or suffering, solely as punitive is a wasted opportunity for self-reflection and growth. "Rather than understanding suffering as the work of a vindictive or sadistic God," Dan tells me, "we need to think of *yisurim* as God's way of communicating that some area of our lives needs spiritual work of one form or another done." Coming from a guy who is a cancer survivor, this notion at least deserves a fair hearing. Dan directs me first to Deuteronomy 8:15, "So you shall know in your heart that the way a man disciplines his child, so your God disciplines you." And then to Deuteronomy 14:1, which opens with "You are children of your God."

Jewish liturgy does indeed refer to the Creator as *Avinu Malkeinu* or "Our Father, Our King." I myself opened this book by saying that I wanted to explore my relationship with my father and with my Father "Who Art in Heaven." And yet I am resistant to the notion that my Heavenly Father uses suffering to telegraph the need for spiritual work. Or that my earthly father was indifferent to the hurt his going away caused.

Have I been too tough on the Pater?

One late winter afternoon, I am sitting with a local family therapist in a neighborhood café. She hears my story and comes to the conclusion that I have objectified the Pater; that I related to him as if he was devoid of feeling. I have done this as a way of insulating myself from being hurt. Obviously, there's no shortage of children who've been emotionally wounded by their parents, she says. Becoming a parent is a way to redeem the parent-child relationship, a way to prove that you are not the same as your parents; that you learned from your own experience as a child, and are better equipped for parenting. Being childless precludes me from avoiding my father's mistakes – or my mother's for that matter. That's what feels unresolved, she tells me.

One of the best things that's happened to me in the course of this journey is that it has served as a catalyst for rethinking the Pater. Perhaps the Pater I've come to discover in my adulthood threatens my old narrative, a narrative that I have a lot invested in. Perhaps my childhood memories of my father – and how I perceived him for the thirty years we didn't communicate – were skewed. Perhaps the family papers and correspondence that I used to reconstruct our history tell only a fragment of the story. The truth is I know so little about my parents' marriage, and recall so little about the relationship I had with my father before he went away.

The Pater I know as an adult is a frail elderly man – an aged zealot, still insistent in his piety, still unfathomable, but not ferocious, not without warmth, and even self-deprecating about his own feebleness.

My revisionist perspective is partly the outcome of the changing dynamics of our relationship. I'm now beyond middle age. The Pater is very old. We are becoming comfortable spending time together.

On this journey I have worked on forgiving myself for being childless, and my father for being absent when I was a child. The sweetest revenge is forgiveness.[2] It is also the best balm.

Time is short. I'm past judging.

---

2. This quote is attributed to I. Friedmann, *Imre Bina*, (1912) and quoted in Joseph L. Baron, *A Treasury of Jewish Quotations* (Northvale, NJ: J. Aronson, 1985).

Acknowledgments

This book would not have been written had I not lost my job. Around the time Hurricane Sandy struck the US East Coast in October 2012, I got word that the projects I'd been working on in Israel for the New York-based Tikvah Fund were being phased out or "reconfigured." Roger Hertog and Eric Cohen appreciated my work and diligence, but my services were no longer needed. It was the soft landing Tikvah provided that allowed me to start work on this book.

The beginning of a book project can be a nervous time. My Tikvah colleague Ran Baratz is not a man who allows sentimentality to cloud his judgment. I told him what I wanted to write about, figuring if he didn't think it was a good idea – it probably wasn't. He was encouraging. I cross paths only infrequently with Ben Balint, the author and book reviewer. All the same, he was one of the first people I turned to. He gave me generous pointers on book writing, agents, and publishers. Our friend Sally Berkovic, the author and London-based Jewish community professional, was encouraging. She read the original proposal and offered an unadorned reaction that kept me on the right path. I also benefited from subsequent discussions with Sally and her erudite husband Rabbi Jonathan Fishburn.

It was a pivotal meeting with Sheryl Abbey, then working for Toby Press and now an independent publicist, that really kick-started this project. Her belief in the viability of the idea and her willingness to champion the project encouraged me to move forward. I am grateful to my publisher, Matthew Miller of Toby, for embracing the idea, being patient with my tardiness, and bringing out this book. Early on, my friend the prolific author Morris Rosenthal gave me practical advice, level-headed encouragement, told me which pitfalls to avoid, and helped me improve on the book proposal. He also commented helpfully on an early draft.

Howard Weber is my friend and longstanding general counsel. He and Gail Weber read the penultimate draft, offered useful comments, and lots of encouragement. They warmly supported the book idea from its inception. Encouragement – emotional, professional, and spiritual – came in generous dollops from Rabbi Avraham Feder, Neal Kozodoy, Suzi Garment, David Horovitz, Anna Olswanger, Jonathan Tobin, Rev. Elwood McQuaid, Miriam Talmor, Allen Einhorn, and Nomi Payton.

I cannot adequately express my gratitude to Naomi Danis, managing editor of *Lilith* magazine, who read the draft with her practiced eye, and provided me with a laundry list of fixes that immeasurably improved the product. She read past passages that surely annoyed her political sensibilities, propelled by her innate kindness and generosity. All the while, she encouraged the project and gave me useful contacts and suggestions to pursue. Several other friends and colleagues read the manuscript, returning it to me with helpful suggestions and thought-provoking criticisms. In this regard, I want to express appreciation to Dr. George Mandel, Rabbi Matthew Wagner, and Debi Pinto. I benefited greatly from the wisdom of Lee Wolfe, Saul Singer, Ruthie Blum, and Rabbi Isaac Lifshitz.

My editor at Toby Press, Sara Sherbill, not only line edited the manuscript, she also offered sage advice about what worked and what didn't. Her involvement made this a better book. I thank her for her diligence, professionalism, and encouragement. I also owe a debt of gratitude to my old colleague Esther Rosenfeld, line editor extraordinaire, for proofing the manuscript. And to Suzanne Libenson and Tomi Mager of Toby Press for the tender care they took in seeing this book to fruition. Holding it all together was Toby's editor in chief Gila Fine, whose talents I can frankly say I recognized long ago.

My friend Bob Cohen not only read the original proposal and draft and provided helpful ongoing feedback, he was also my lunch partner throughout the project, putting up with my kvetching about the book and everything else.

They may not know it but the camaraderie of the fellows in the (formerly) Middle Aged Men's Book Club of Jerusalem also helped spur me on. No one did more to bring this project to fruition than Judy Montagu Fossaner, my editor, mentor, and understanding friend. Judy read and re-read every page and immeasurably improved the final product.

My father-in-law, David Clayton, passed away several months before this book was completed. In his unfussy British manner he was thoroughly supportive and encouraging. One afternoon, at Meir Hospital in Kfar Saba, as we sat taking in the sun, out of the blue he asked if I had decided on a title for the book. I showed him what I had. He nodded as if to say, "Good. Carry on." Zena Clayton, my dear mother-in-law, supported my decision to write this book and cheered me on. She read the final manuscript when staying with us – for the last time it turned out – during Rosh HaShana, 5775. True to character, she gave it her full attention and she gave me her full blessing.

In the process of writing this book, my father's daughter – my half-sister, whom I call Esti – became my friend. We come from such different worlds and never met until we were both adults. But the affection and respect with which she treats the Pater has endeared her and her family to me.

To my wife and partner, Lisa, I can only say: You are the best thing that has happened to me. I could not have started, much less completed this book without you. But I understate.

Let the record show that I alone am responsible for what is written here. There was plenty of advice that I didn't take. At the end of the day, I followed my own counsel.

I hope my mother would have approved.

Elliot Jager
Jerusalem
Summer 2015

The fonts used in this book are from the Garamond family